# WOMEN
# AMPLIFIED

# WOMEN AMPLIFIED

20 YEARS OF INSIGHTS FROM
TRAILBLAZING LEADERS
FROM THE STAGE OF THE
TEXAS CONFERENCE FOR WOMEN

COMPILED AND EDITED BY
LISA BENNETT

GREENLEAF
BOOK GROUP PRESS

Published by Greenleaf Book Group Press
Austin, Texas
www.gbgpress.com

Distributed by Greenleaf Book Group

For ordering information or special discounts for bulk purchases, please contact Greenleaf Book Group at PO Box 91869, Austin, TX 78709, 512.891.6100.

Design and composition by Greenleaf Book Group and Kim Lance
Cover design by Greenleaf Book Group and Kim Lance
©iStock/Getty Images Plus/rootstocks

Publisher's Cataloging-in-Publication data is available.

Print ISBN: 978-1-62634-691-8

eBook ISBN: 978-1-62634-692-5

Part of the Tree Neutral® program, which offsets the number of trees consumed in the production and printing of this book by taking proactive steps, such as planting trees in direct proportion to the number of trees used: www.treeneutral.com

TreeNeutral

Printed in the United States of America on acid-free paper

19 20 21 22 23 24 25   10 9 8 7 6 5 4 3 2 1

First Edition

*This book is dedicated
to the 107,480 women and men
who have participated in
the Texas Conference for Women
since its founding in 2000.*

## ACKNOWLEDGMENTS

This book is, in itself, an expression of gratitude to those who shared the inspiring, insightful words quoted here; the thousands of women and men who worked to make twenty years of the Texas Conference for Women possible; and the more than 100,000 Texas women who participated and brought it all to life.

Specifically on behalf of the Texas Conference for Women team, thank you to our exceptional board: President Carla Piñeyro Sublett, and Directors Sabrina T. Brown, Bobbi Dangerfield, Tamara Fields, Jane Gasdaska, Carol McGarah, and Lisa McLin. Deep appreciation also goes to our wonderful past board members: Jan Bullock, Cassandra Carr, Debbie Dunnam, Nene Foxhall, Kathleen Lucas, Jan Newton, Karen Quintos, Kathy Sosa, Alejandra De La Vega Foster, Norine Yukon—and Johnita Jones, who led the board for more than a decade. And of course, warm thanks to Anita Perry, who was for many years a grand ambassador and gracious host.

I would also like to share how much I respect and appreciate the entire outstanding Texas Conference for Women team. For their contributions to this book, I'm especially thankful to Danielle Leshinski, Isha St. Amour, and Lindsay Reinhardt. For everything they do to cultivate this special community every day, thanks to Jess Black, Amy Cooper, Marlyse Fant, Carolyn Gan, Laura Hilgeman, Jasmine Jacobs, Rachael Lange, Wendy Morris, Will Hornaday, Denise McVeigh, Shuronda Robinson, Sarah Shulman, Michelle Voetberg, and Miranda Wicker. Thanks also to Wendi Aarons. A very special thanks to Laurie Dalton White, leader of all things Conferences for Women. If not for her, none of this would have come to be.

Deep gratitude also goes to our immensely valued sponsors who have made this conference and book possible. Appreciation, in addition, to Elizabeth Brown for her enthusiastic support and generous feedback, Sally Garland for her caring and skillful editing, and the whole Greenleaf Book Group team.

Finally, thanks to you and every woman who picks up this book—for receiving these words and doing what you do to keep them alive.

# Contents

# Knowledge. Strength. Confidence. Inspiration. Power: Why This Book Came to Be

hen women come together, they bring the potential for something special—possibly transformative—to occur. Most of us have experienced that magic moment at some time in our lives, and if we're fortunate, many times. When we connect and share our truth, our experiences, and our wisdom with another woman, we suddenly know that something more and better is possible—in ourselves and in the world.

We are relational beings, after all. As the emotional intelligence expert Daniel Goleman, my co-author on the book *Ecoliterate*, has written, "We are wired to connect." This idea applies, of course, to both men and women. And with full deference to the limits of generalizations and sweeping statements such as the following, here I go: It is widely accepted that women are just a little more wired to connect. We get a great deal out of being in each other's company and talking together.

So, if good things happen when two, three, or four women come together, what happens when 7,500 do? Or, over twenty years' time, more than 100,000? That is the story of the Texas Conference for Women, which was founded in 2000—a time when there was nowhere near the number of women's conferences as there are today. The feeling of being in a room with that many women is something that truly has to be experienced to be understood. The unforgettable and visceral sense of power and possibility that comes from standing among thousands of professional women, aspiring women, inspirational women, struggling women, young women, old women, women of all political persuasions, and women united by a commitment to personal and professional growth is an experience that changes you.

But not everyone can have an experience such as this—nor perhaps have it when they need it most. That is why this book came to be. It's not intended as a substitute for the experience of being at such a conference—because that is not something that can be conveyed through words on a page alone. But what can be shared, and what this book aims to offer, is a distillation of the wisdom, wit, insights, and inspirations that have been shared at this pioneering conference over the past two decades.

Think of the pages that follow as an opportunity to visit—whenever you feel you need to—with remarkable women (and some very supportive men) from across America and beyond. Among them:

National Book Award winner **Isabel Allende**

Nobel Peace Laureate **Leymah Gbowee**

Pulitzer Prize–winning reporter **Sheryl WuDunn**

Emmy- and Peabody Award–winning journalist **Maria Hinojosa**

The magnificent Academy (and many other)
Award–winning actress **Viola Davis**

Olympian, soccer star, and activist **Abby Wambach**

**Ruth Simmons,** the daughter of sharecroppers who became
the president of Brown University

International human rights attorney **Amal Clooney**

The late Governor **Ann Richards**

Global philanthropist **Melinda French Gates**

**Martha Beck,** one of America's best-known life coaches

Mega entrepreneur **Martha Stewart**

**Nancy Brinker,** who built the world's largest nonprofit
source of funding for the fight against breast cancer
after her sister died of the disease

Happiness experts **Shawn Achor** and **Gretchen Rubin**

Psychologist **Adam Grant**

**Brené Brown,** who has taught
so many about vulnerability and courage

**Charlotte Beers** of Ogilvy & Mather Worldwide

**Carly Fiorina** of Hewlett-Packard

**Sallie Krawcheck** of Smith Barney and
Merrill Lynch Wealth Management

**Pat Mitchell** of PBS and CNN Productions

**Sheryl Sandberg** of Facebook

**Cathie Black** of Hearst Magazines and *USA Today*

**Vernā Myers,** vice president of Inclusion Strategy at Netflix

These people are included here because they have important
things to say about believing in yourself, designing the work–life
balance that suits you, cultivating inclusion, dreaming big, finding courage, taking chances, growing from challenges and sur-
passing limitations, owning your influence, seeing possibilities

and making change, and—perhaps, above all—becoming the women the world needs now.

## Becoming the Women the World Needs Now

It's no secret that this is an important time for women—in Texas and across America. We are living in a moment of profound change and significant uncertainty. Times like these can be unsettling, but they can also be full of potential. An analysis of all the issues related to women in the workplace is beyond the scope of this book, but we can't fail to note some key points about the current state of women in the workforce.

### *More People Support Gender Equality Than Don't*

In the words of the indomitable Gloria Steinem, an observer of and leader in women's rights for more than fifty years, "For the first time in my lifetime, we have majority support for all the basic issues that the women's movement has cared about historically and that we look forward to."[1] More than two-thirds of Americans believe in gender equality at work and at home—up from just one-quarter—according to a forty-year analysis of the General Social Survey conducted by the University of Chicago.[2]

### *The Majority of Americans Have No Preference about the Gender of Their Bosses*

In fact, men are significantly more likely than women to *lack* a preference.[3] Most see men and women as equally capable, and among those who see differences in women's and men's leadership styles, 62 percent say neither is better, while 22 percent say women generally have the better approach.[4] Women are also viewed as significantly better at creating safe and respectful workplaces.[5]

### A Record-Breaking Number of Women Are Running For and Winning Public Office

In the 2018 midterm elections, thirty-six new women won seats in the House of Representatives, bringing the total to 102, the largest number ever. As of this writing, a woman, Speaker of the House Nancy Pelosi, holds the third-highest office in the nation. And, as of this writing, six women have announced their candidacy for president.

### Women Are Making Significant Inroads into Traditionally Male-Dominated Professions

For example, women's employment grew more than 10 percent in construction, mining, and transportation and utilities—some of the fastest-growing fields in the United States.[6] There has also been a growth of women in STEM (science, technology, engineering, and math) fields, according to a 2019 LinkedIn study that found more women entered STEM over the past forty years than any other field.[7]

### *Women Are Getting Richer*

Worldwide, private wealth held by women grew from $34 trillion to $51 trillion between 2010 and 2015, according to the Boston Consulting Group.[8] In the United States, women control more than 60 percent of the private wealth and are expected to control two-thirds of it by 2030. The number of wealthy women is growing at twice the rate of wealthy men. And 45 percent of the nation's millionaires are women.[9]

## The Other Side to the Story

But there is, of course, another side to the story.

- A persistent and sizeable gender pay gap still exists. In 2018, women earned 85 percent of what men earned—meaning, a woman would have to work 39 more days every year to earn what a man did in 2018.[10]

- As dramatically brought to life by the #MeToo movement, a full 60 percent of women say they have experienced "unwanted sexual attention, sexual coercion, sexually crude conduct, or sexist comments" in the workplace.[11]

- And women are wildly, and increasingly, underrepresented in top positions of leadership. In 2018, only twenty-four (or 4.8 percent) out of all chief executives at Fortune 500 companies were women in 2018—down from a record of thirty-two in 2017. In May 2019, this number increased again to thirty-three women—which is a record high, although still not representative of women in the workplace.

Many complex factors contribute to the persistence of these indicators of gender inequity in the workplace.

- Inequity in hiring is a significant factor—with men being more likely to be hired into manager-level jobs than women, according to the 2018 LeanIn.Org and McKinsey Women in the Workplace study. "This early inequality has a profound impact on the talent pipeline," the report states. "Starting at the manager level, there are significantly fewer women to promote from within and significantly fewer women at the right experience level to hire in from the outside."[12]

- Microaggressions are another factor cited by the LeanIn.Org and McKinsey Women in the Workplace study, and these aggressions can take many forms, such as women having their judgment questioned in their area of expertise, being forced to provide more evidence of competence than men have to do, and being addressed in a less than professional way in public and private settings.

- Another factor is the double bind that women experience in the workplace, a phenomenon observed by Katherine W. Phillips, a professor of organizational management at Columbia University and others. "If they're perceived as nice and warm and nurturing, as they're expected to be, they don't show what it takes to move into a leadership position. But when they take charge to get things done, they're often seen as angrier or more aggressive than men."[13]

These means of exclusion serve no one—not men, or women, or our workplaces. Research has overwhelmingly shown that diverse teams lead to improved productivity, enhanced problem solving, and increased innovation. Diverse teams are also better able to serve a diverse consumer base that is increasingly dominated by "belief-driven" buyers who want to support brands that stand for something.[14] A positive corporate culture is one that values diversity and inclusion, and it is a critical component in companies' quests to attract and retain top talent in today's world.

## Looking Back— and Ahead: Focusing on the Big Picture

So, what are we to make of this moment for women? You will see that several of the successful women quoted in this book make it clear that it is crucial that we keep our focus on the big picture. We have to keep track of how far we've come and who we have to thank for that. We also have to keep track of how far we still have to go, and how we must look to ourselves and our male allies to create workplaces that work for all.

In that spirit, it is both telling and heartening to consider the story of one woman, not quoted in this book, but without whom neither this book nor the conference at which all these women were speakers would have come to be.

More than twenty years ago, Laurie Dalton White was a new mom with a two-week-old son and on maternity leave from her work at the public interest group Public Strategies. Some years before (with no small amount of skepticism), Laurie had attended a women's conference on the West Coast at the urging of a colleague. She came away thinking she had never before experienced anything like it—or the palpable sense of energy that came with being at such an event. The following year, she invited a few other women to the conference. One young woman just starting out said just being there was life changing and had helped her find her calling.

"I saw how it impacted everyone—in big ways and little ways," Laurie recently recalled. "I knew how powerful the experience of community was." She also knew back then that there was nothing like it in Texas. So, Laurie started reaching out. Once she realized how few women's conferences there really were, she decided she would need to affiliate the event with statewide officeholders who could provide it with the visibility and credibility it needed. She contacted First Lady Laura Bush (who was about to join her husband, then the Governor of Texas, in a presidential campaign), Lieutenant Governor Rick Perry, and Representative Pete Laney (who was Speaker of the House and a Democrat), thinking the best possible conference would be a bipartisan one.

All three accepted her offer and agreed to be part of the new event. Anita Perry signed on to host, and she toured the state with Laurie to help raise visibility (a role she would continue to play for the fifteen years her husband served as governor). Gaye Polan and Monica Hearn from Governor Perry's office also were both early champions of the conference.

Six months in, Laurie sought a little more help and recruited a single assistant and a program director, Amy Cooper, who, twenty years later, is still with the Conference for Women. She raised a half million dollars from sponsors, and within a year, the first Texas Conference for Women was held—in October of 2000. It attracted 2,800 women.

Today, Laurie's children are in college, and she and her team have built the largest nationwide network of women's conferences in the country that include not only the pioneering Texas Conference for Women, but also the Massachusetts Conference for Women, the Pennsylvania Conference for Women, and the Watermark Conference for Women Silicon Valley. More than 45,000 women participate in these conferences every year. In fact, these events have become so popular that Laurie is working to expand access by offering new events such as Opening Nights and Workplace Summits and providing online digital programming.

As former First Lady Anita Perry said, "Just like all of us ladies, the conference just keeps getting better with age."

Yet today Laurie says she is often asked whether women still need conferences of their own. Her answer is *absolutely*—because the value of coming together as a community and supporting each other is certainly as important now as it has ever been. "I want people to have options. I want my son to have the options my daughter does. I want my daughter to have the options my son does. I want everyone's kids to have options. My parents instilled in me a strong sense of fairness."

Perhaps a worthy final thought is that if one woman, driven by a belief in fairness, can spark that much change, innovation, and inspiration in twenty years, what can all of us, individually and collectively, achieve over the next twenty? That is the story we will write as we move forward from this moment when women are coming together—in marches, online, at the voting booth, and at conferences—like never before.

My hope is that you accept this book as both a celebration of what happens when women come together and a handbook of inspiration for the years of transformation, growth, and progress ahead.

# 1

# Assume You Belong— and Believe In Yourself

. . . . . . . . .

# SARA MARTINEZ TUCKER

*"We're multitaskers, we're nurturers, we're empathetic, and we ought to take advantage of that. But what can take us to that place where we can feel that we've fully achieved?*

*"I think we have to find an ability to speak and be heard, and that will only happen when you assume you belong."*

. . . . . . . . . . . .

Sara is the Chairman of the University of Texas System Board of Regents. She was Under Secretary of Education, and President and CEO of the Hispanic Scholarship Fund. She was once told by a college counselor that she was "not college material." She's a Texan.

# JERI CALLAWAY

*"Life is really about some very simple basics: the core values, our characters, and what we really stand for. Sometimes simplicity and the basics can be the most important guidance for all of us, whether that's in our personal lives or whether that's in our business careers."*

. . . . . . . . . . . .

Jeri Callaway is the former Senior VP and General Manager of Hewlett-Packard. She is currently a business consultant in private practice and lives in Houston.

# MARY WILSON

*"I always thought I was a star in the background. So, it doesn't matter where you stand or what you do, as long as you believe in yourself."*

. . . . . . . . . . . .

Mary was the founding member of the Supremes and remained its longest member over eighteen years. She has three solo albums, two best-selling memoirs, and a forthcoming book, *Supreme Glamour,* to her credit. She was a United States State Department Cultural Ambassador.

# CATHIE BLACK

*"Here's what I learned about adversity and leading from really challenging times: You have to project confidence. It doesn't matter how you feel on the inside. You've got to project confidence."*

. . . . . . . . . . . .

Cathie is currently an angel investor. She served as President and Chairman of Hearst Magazines and as President and Publisher of *USA Today.* She was the first woman publisher of a weekly consumer magazine, *New York Magazine.* She is *The New York Times* best-selling author of *Basic Black: The Essential Guide for Getting Ahead at Work.*

# VIOLA DAVIS

*"What I've decided is—(like Moses, who was a stutterer and then had to lead everybody out of Egypt, and he was like, 'I stutter. You want me to do that?'), I say that I am broken and I am 'the stutterer.'*

*"But my sweet elixir is I am willing. I am awoke. I have left my safe place of feeling less than—and there are days that I still do.*

*"But, by God, I know that I have a higher purpose, and there are moments, days, months that go by of pure joy and elation and signs that say: 'You know what? I'm doing pretty good.'*

*"Those moments keep me alive. They keep me in my meaning."*

. . . . . . . . . . . .

Viola is an actress and producer and the winner of the Academy Award, an Emmy, a Golden Globe, a Screen Actors Guild award, and a Tony Award. She is the author of the children's book *Corduroy Takes a Bow*. She is also a skydiver.

# LISA NIEMI SWAYZE

*"One of my favorite songs is 'I Believe In Me,' and I can sing it with gusto and get all teary-eyed. But when I back off the song, I'm going, I don't know how to do that. How do I believe in me? There are no steps for me to follow. I just don't know how to do that.*

*"But I know how to get out of bed in the morning. That I can*

*do. And for many people, when all is lost, sometimes we need to go outside ourselves for guidance and go to a higher spiritual power . . . And it's interesting how you make wiser decisions when you have something on your side supporting you."*

. . . . . . . . . . . .

Lisa is an actress and director, and *The New York Times* best-selling author of *Worth Fighting For: Love, Loss, and Moving Forward*. She was born in Houston. She's a pilot and the widow of Patrick Swayze.

# CHARLOTTE BEERS

*"You can transform the reception you get from complex, skeptical, and difficult audiences if you can speak from the center of who you are about something you believe greatly."*

. . . . . . . . . . . .

Charlotte is the former Chairman and CEO of Ogilvy & Mather Worldwide and the former Undersecretary for Public Diplomacy and Public Affairs. She was the first woman to appear on the cover of *Fortune*, and is the author of *I'd Rather Be in Charge: A Legendary Business Leader's Roadmap for Achieving Pride, Power, and Joy at Work*. She was born in Texas.

# DR. JEN ARNOLD

*"I tried from an early age to be realistic about my capabilities and know what those capabilities were. But although I knew what my capabilities were, everybody else may not have.*

*"So, part of my job of achieving my dreams was to educate people about what my capabilities really were."*

. . . . . . . . . . . .

Jen is a neonatologist and the medical director of the Simulation Center at Texas Children's Hospital and Assistant Professor of Pediatrics at Baylor College of Medicine in Houston. She is a co-star of TLC's *The Little Couple,* and co-author of *Think Big: Overcoming Obstacles with Optimism.*

# SARA MARTINEZ TUCKER

*"Think about the people you respect. Think about the people you admire. Think about the people who you listen to, male or female. You respect where they are. You respect where they came from, and you respect what they're doing. And . . . they respect where they are, too. That's the gap that we have to close. We have to assume we belong."*

# 2

# Change Your Situation, Change the World

. . . . . . . .

# GRETCHEN RUBIN

"*It's very tempting to think, 'I would be happier if other people would behave properly,' and to come up with a long list of resolutions for other people to follow.*

"*Unfortunately, it doesn't work like that. The only person you can change is yourself. What I found is that when I change, a relationship changes. When I change, the atmosphere of my home changes. So, I could make larger changes by just focusing on myself.*"

. . . . . . . . . . . . .

Gretchen Rubin is *The New York Times* best-selling author of *The Happiness Project* and, most recently, of *Outer Order, Inner Calm: Declutter and Organize to Make More Room for Happiness.* She is a Yale Law School graduate who clerked for former Supreme Court Justice Sandra Day O'Connor and has walked arm in arm with the Dalai Lama.

# LEYMAH GBOWEE

"*My mother says I'm like the one who would never test the water but dives in headfirst, because if you think too much, you lose your steam.*

"*It is possible, people, for us to make a change. It is possible for us to turn our upside-down world upright. We took on a dictator, and we decided we were not going to stop as a group of women.*

*"When the winds and the waves were against us, we threatened to strip naked. When the winds and the waves were against us, and without the benefit of arms, we barricaded men with guns into a hall, held hands, and said, 'You can't come out.' When the winds and waves were against us, we went to the UN and told them, 'You are not doing this right.'*

*"'We live here; we know the solution to this problem.'*

*"'When the winds and the waves were against us, we went out there and mobilized women and made history by electing Africa's first female president. We all have the power in us to change the tide.'"*

. . . . . . . . . . . .

Leymah is a Nobel Peace Prize Laureate and the founder of the Gbowee Peace Foundation. She is Executive Director of the Women, Peace, and Security Program at Columbia University, and the author of *Mighty Be Our Powers: How Sisterhood, Prayer, and Sex Changed a Nation at War.*

# KATHLEEN DAELEMANS

*"If you don't like who you're working with, make change. Stay as long as you need to. And then, when you know it's time for you to go, go."*

. . . . . . . . . . . .

Kathleen is a chef and the host of the Food Network show *Cooking Thin.* She is also a *New York Times* best-selling author of *Cooking Thin with Chef Kathleen*. Her first job was as a counter girl at Henry Yee's Chinese carryout, where by observing cooks in the kitchen, she could eventually make 600 egg rolls a night.

## LEIGH ANNE TUOHY

*"You can make a difference. The power of one is huge.*

*"Your children can make a difference; they're little mirror images of you."*

. . . . . . . . . . .

Leigh Anne is best known as the legal guardian of Michael Oher, who was the subject of Michael Lewis's book, *The Blind Side,* and the 2009 movie of the same name. Portrayed by Sandra Bullock in the film, Leigh Anne is an entrepreneur, an interior designer, and the author of *In a Heartbeat: Sharing the Power of Cheerful Giving.*

## ISABEL ALLENDE

*"We are going to change the world, ladies. I promise you that."*

. . . . . . . . . . .

Novelist, feminist, philanthropist—and one of the most widely read authors in the world, Isabel Allende counts her most significant achievements as "the love I share with a few people— especially my family—and the ways in which I have tried to help others." She was inducted into the American Academy of Arts and Letters and awarded the 2014 Presidential Medal of Freedom.

## LEYMAH GBOWEE

*"The world is waiting for you to stand up and make a fool out of yourself in order to change the tide.*

*"Because you see, in this world that we live in, these sensible things don't make sense anymore.*

*"It's the crazy things that will bring our world upright. Join me. You have the power. Let's make it possible for some girl, some woman, to dream."*

## LINDA CLIATT-WAYMAN

*"If you are near the end of one assignment, pondering a new one, or waiting on one, and you are standing in one spot and afraid to move left or right, afraid about what would happen if you choose left over right or right over left, do yourself a favor: Do not worry about directional order.*

*"Just be sure to move. Move one step closer to fulfill that dream you have always had for yourself. Visualize it day and night. See yourself doing exactly what you always wanted to do. You got it. Go get it. Think like an entrepreneur and take some risk. It will be worth it."*

Linda was the principal of the Philadelphia's Strawberry Mansion High School, which was profiled by Diane Sawyer and her team for *ABC World News Tonight* and *Nightline*. Under her leadership, the school was removed from the federal Persistently Dangerous Schools List, and test scores improved every year since she took over. She is the author of *Lead Fearlessly, Love Hard: Finding Your Purpose and Putting It to Work.*

# 3

# Connect. And Everything Becomes Better

# SHAWN ACHOR

*"If you're viewing a mountain by yourself, your brain perceives a mountain that is 10–20% steeper than a mountain of the same height you perceive while standing next to a friend who's going to climb it with you."*

. . . . . . . . . . . .

Shawn is an author and popular speaker known for his advocacy of positive psychology. Among his books are *The New York Times* best seller, *The Happiness Advantage,* and his most recent *Big Potential: How Transforming the Pursuit of Success Raises Our Achievement, Happiness, and Well-Being.* His wife and sister are also happiness experts. He lives in Texas.

# CANDY CHANG

*"I think that when we feel fear or anxiety or confusion, we often do our very best to hide it from others. But what if we could make more safe places to share? There's great power in knowing that you're not alone: You're not alone as you're trying to make sense of your life, and you're not the only one who feels like they're barely keeping it together."*

. . . . . . . . . . . .

Candy is an artist, designer, and urban planner—and leader in participatory public art. She is the creator of the project, "Before I Die," which began after she lost someone she loved and painted the side of an abandoned house in New Orleans with chalkboard paint and stenciled the sentence: "Before I die I want to _____." Within a day, it was covered in colorful chalk dreams. Since then, more than 4,000 "Before I Die" walls have been created in more than seventy countries. Her latest participatory public installation is *A Monument for the Anxious and Hopeful.*

## CARLY FIORINA

*"When people work together, everything is possible."*

. . . . . . . . . . . .

Former CEO of Hewlett-Packard (HP) and the first woman to ever lead a Fortune 500 company, Carly is a former candidate for US President and the author of *Find Your Way: Unleash Your Power and Highest Potential.* She began her career as a secretary. Carly was born in Austin.

## NINA TASSLER

*"It was in the insanely competitive, egocentric world of Holly-wood talent agencies that I found a wonderful mentor, a man with whom I remain friends to this day. He taught me there is no limit to what you can do if you don't mind who gets the credit.*

*"This is a wonderfully liberating idea. Because if taking credit and ownership is a driving principle, you will miss out*

*on the experiential quality of working, the joys of learning and collaborating."*

. . . . . . . . . . . .

Nina is the former Chairman of CBS Entertainment and responsible for shows such as *The Good Wife, The Big Bang Theory, ER,* and others. She is the author of *What I Told My Daughter: Lessons from Leaders on Raising the Next Generation of Empowered Women.*

## ABBY WAMBACH

*"As women, we all have to stick together. We all have to be a part of this bigger team, whether we're here in Austin or in different cities around the country. We women have to stick together in order to grow, in order to gain headway and ground in the things that we want to accomplish in this world."*

. . . . . . . . . . . .

Abby is a soccer icon, a two-time Olympic gold medalist, and winner of the 2015 FIFA Women's World Cup. She has scored more international goals than any woman or man in history. She is an activist for equality and inclusion, and the author of the 2019 book, *Wolfpack: How to Come Together, Unleash Our Power, and Change the Game.* Her autobiography, *Forward,* released in September 2016, became a *New York Times* best seller.

# PATRICIA ARQUETTE

*"We know that when men support women, change comes ten times faster."*

· · · · · · · · · · · ·

Patricia has won an Academy Award, a BAFTA Award, a Critics' Choice Award, a Golden Globe, and a Screen Actors Guild Award. A self-described troublemaker, she fights for fair pay and passage of the Equal Rights Amendment.

# SALLIE KRAWCHECK

*"Your network matters. And research shows that we ladies don't have nearly the network that the gentlemen do.*

*"It's one of the reasons—it's the reason—the guys start to pull ahead of us in their thirties in promotions. It's not ability. It's not hard work. You've seen it. It's network.*

*"Did you know that network has been cited as the Number One unwritten rule of success in business? And did you know that your next business opportunity is more likely to come from a loose connection, somebody you just talk to a couple times a year, than from a close colleague or friend?*

*"That's because that one loose connection is one of many seeds you plant that can be the difference between hearing about an opportunity, a research breakthrough, a board position, a new job, a startup that's threatening your company, and not."*

Known as one of the most senior women to have worked on Wall Street, Sallie has served as CEO of Smith Barney and Merrill Lynch Wealth Management, and CFO at Citigroup. She currently is CEO and co-founder of Ellevest, a digital financial advisor for women; the owner and chair of the Ellevate Network; and a *Wall Street Journal*–best-selling author of *Own It: The Power of Women at Work.* She's also a basketball fan.

## SHAWN ACHOR

*"Social connection is the greatest predictor of your long-term levels of happiness. It's the greatest predictor of your long-term levels of success. And we just found out social connection is as predictive of how long you will end up living as obesity, high blood pressure, or smoking."*

## CARLY FIORINA

*"Seek out the people who will take a chance on you. There are people who won't take a chance on you—to heck with them. They're not worth your time. Seek out the people who will take a chance on you; there are plenty of those in the world."*

# ADAM GRANT

*"The time you spend solving other people's problems increases your ability to solve your own problem and your organization's problems."*

. . . . . . . . . . .

Adam is an organizational psychologist and a Wharton School professor. He is the host of *WorkLife* podcast and author of *Originals: How Non-Conformists Move the World*. He is also co-author with Sheryl Sandberg of *Option B: Facing Adversity, Building Resilience, and Finding Joy*.

# SALLIE KRAWCHECK

*"In business, a sponsor matters. Notice I didn't say mentor.*

*"A mentor's good. A mentor is someone who's there to answer your question and advise you. A sponsor is a super mentor, someone who deeply believes in your ability and who fights for you, fights for that raise for you, fights for that promotion for you, fights for that new project for you, fights against your getting fired. We women tend to be over-mentored and under-sponsored."*

# CHARLOTTE BEERS

"*Women say to me they don't like office politics; politics are messy relationships.*

"*You've got to get in the game. You can't step aside 'til everybody becomes nice again. They get messy going up the ladder. Order succumbs to chaos. Loyal teams that you built and loved are replaced by hostile ones. Why? Because you're making changes. You're trying to make something happen. You're trying to fix that which is broken, and you're no longer adored and popular.*

"*You're in charge. This is not easy . . . In order to handle these more challenging relationships, you need two things: . . . You need to know who you are . . . And you also need to know how to be an artful communicator.*"

# ISABEL ALLENDE

"*According to Jean Shinoda Bolen, in her book* The Millionth Circle, *a critical number of women gathering in connected circles can tip the balance of power and end the patriarchy.*"

# SUZE ORMAN

"*When you can connect with the power that is in you, and you can look in the mirror, and you like what is looking back at you, now you are a wealthy woman. Now you are a powerful woman.*

*Now you are a woman who no matter what happens in the economy, no matter what happens anywhere else, nobody can take that power away from you."*

. . . . . . . . . . . .

Suze is a two-time Emmy Award–winning personal finance expert and a #1 *New York Times* best-selling author, most recently of the revised and updated *Women & Money: Be Strong. Be Smart. Be Secure.* She was once a struggling waitress at the Buttercup Café in Berkeley.

# 4

# Design the Work–Life Balance That Works for You

# KAREN HUGHES

*"We all face a tug-of-war to be responsible in our different roles as spouse or father or mother or employee or boss or son or daughter. Life is a series of conflicting demands, and we make choices. The challenge, I think, is to make sure those choices are based on our priorities. We all have to decide what is true and lasting and important to us and use that to ground our decisions.*

*"Saint Augustine used a beautiful phrase called* ordo amoris, *the order of the loves. The most important thing you will do in life is to choose your loves and order them very carefully."*

. . . . . . . . . . . .

Karen is Global Vice Chair of Burson-Marsteller and former Under Secretary of State for Public Diplomacy and Public Affairs in the US Department of State. She was a counselor to President George W. Bush and is the author of *Ten Minutes from Normal*. She lives in Austin, Texas.

# CHARLOTTE BEERS

*"You are not at work the person you are at home. You will find this to be very liberating. Whoever you are at home needs to stay there.*

*"You can be at work and be an edgier, braver, different person. You can use sides and sets of yourself that would not be called on in these other experiences. And don't you think that is part of the reason we love to work?"*

# ANNE-MARIE SLAUGHTER

*"You should put caregiving on your resume. You should say I raised three children, or I took care of my father, or whatever it was. You should put it on your resume, and you should be prepared to talk about what you got out of it.*

*"You grow when you give care. And those skills are transferrable—but more importantly those are just valuable."*

. . . . . . . . . . . .

Anne-Marie is CEO of New America, a think and action tank dedicated to renewing America in the Digital Age. She was the director of policy planning for the United States Department of State, and is the author of the highly influential *The Atlantic* article, *"Why Women Still Can't Have It All."*

# CATHIE BLACK

*"You need a full, rich life to nourish any success that is really worth having. I call it the 360-degree life. Family, friends, fun: These are all as vital as work.*

*"Never, ever forget that you are a whole person in and out of the office. Here's a couple of things that are more import-ant, perhaps, than your job: your health and your well-being, certainly; your sense of purpose; deciding what part of 'all' you want (or, as someone quipped recently, why would you want it all?); contributing to a higher good; and the self-respect that*

*comes from being an authentic person, being real. Having a full plate is great, but having a full life is even better.*

*"Make that your top priority, because when we only measure success by the yardstick of work and its returns (title, salary, perks, status, etc.), we're working against limits, not toward possibilities. We see ourselves as expendable. But when we define success in the fullest definition as a circle of life, we see ourselves as expandable, and that's a state that we want to get to."*

## ANNE-MARIE SLAUGHTER

*"For me, being a mom has been just as important as anything else I've done. I'm also much better at what I do because I'm a mom. Giving care and investing in others is just what we do as managers: You support your people, you guide them, you discipline them if need be, but you also empower them. You let them do what they need to do. That's what being a good parent is about. You know, the investing and the letting go."*

# 5

# Discover Differences. Cultivate Inclusion.

. . . . . . . . . .

# VERNĀ MYERS

*"Diversity is about counting, inclusion is about cultivating. Diversity is about being invited to the party, but inclusion is about being asked to dance.*

*"It's a very different experience to be welcomed in for who you are, and not asked to adapt who you are to the people who've already been there—to do your best impression of a man, basically, or whatever other majority group is controlling and shaping that environment."*

. . . . . . . . . . . .

Vernā is Vice President of Inclusion Strategy at Netflix, and the founder of The Vernā Myers Company. A TED speaker, she is the author of *What If I Say the Wrong Thing? 25 Habits for Culturally Effective People*. She is also a fan of long bike rides.

# BRENÉ BROWN

*"If you're not willing to have conversations about inclusivity, equity, and diversity, you will not be leading in the next five years."*

. . . . . . . . . . . .

Brené is a research professor at the University of Houston and an expert in courage, vulnerability, shame, and empathy. She is the author of four #1 *New York Times* best sellers including, most recently, *Dare to Lead: Brave Work. Tough Conversations.*

*Whole Hearts.* Her TED talk "The Power of Vulnerability" is one of the five most viewed in the world. She is a Texan.

## JOHN GRAY

*"You can be equal and recognize differences. But when everybody's pretending that there are no gender differences, then we get women expected to behave more like men in the workplace, and men expected to behave more like women at home. It's not going to work and it doesn't work.*

*"What we want is greater insight and understanding to help both women and men be their authentic selves. The more the work environment or the personal relationship environment can support the authenticity of who we are, the more your talents, your genius, and your fulfillment will come through."*

. . . . . . . . . . . .

John Gray is an American relationship counselor and the author of the #1 *New York Times* best seller *Men Are from Mars, Women Are from Venus*, and more than twenty other books.

## RUTH SIMMONS

*"So many people who are minorities, or from different countries, or different faiths, come to me, and they say, 'Ruth, I am*

*so tired . . . of having to teach people about my country, or about my hair, or about my religion. I am sick and tired of it, and I'm not going to do it anymore.' That's what they say to me.*

"*Can you imagine what I say to them? I say, 'Get over it!' because our essential, intrinsic duty as human beings is to teach others about who we are. That's how we learn about the complexity of the world that God has created—by meeting people, by learning from them.*"

. . . . . . . . . . . .

Ruth served as president of both Smith College and Brown University and is the first black woman to lead an Ivy League institution. She is now President of Prairie View A&M University. In 2002, *Newsweek* selected her as a Ms. Woman of the Year and in 2001, *Time* magazine named her as America's best college president. She's the native Texan daughter of a sharecropper.

## VERNĀ MYERS

"*What does it mean to create inclusion? What does it mean to actually give people a sense that they're respected, that they're represented, that their ideas are solicited, that their opportunities are there and possible for them to show their best? Well, it means several things. One thing it means is that we have to be okay with noticing differences.*

"*Being colorblind or difference-blind was a great idea. But in order to move diversity forward, we've got to notice who isn't included, who isn't at the table, who is underrepresented, whose voices we aren't hearing. What we really need to be is difference-conscious and difference-competent. These are the new skills."*

## LEIGH ANNE TUOHY

*"We need to get involved. We need to make a difference. We need to make sure that people don't fall through the cracks. Change the face of Houston. Change the face of Texas. Change the complexion of the United States of America. Do something different. Help someone."*

## BRENÉ BROWN

*"If you have conversations about race, class, gender, sexual orientation, and gender expression, you're going to get your ass handed to you. You're going to get called out in the most uncomfortable way about your blind spots. And the more privileged you are, the more you're going to get called out.*

*"And it's going to be hard and maybe painful. I've done it a hundred times, sometimes in public. It's some of the most painful work I've ever done. But to opt out of these difficult conversations because it makes you uncomfortable is the definition of privilege. We can't do that. We've got to lean in.*

*"I'll tell you my tactic. I would say, 'Look. I don't know what's*

going on. [But] something's going on around race and gender and our team, and it's getting in the way of good work.

"I'm about a C+ facilitating this conversation. We can do it with me facilitating, or we can bring in someone who's a solid A who's trained in it. But what we're going [to] do is we're going [to] keep talking about it until we've figured it out.'"

# 6

# Dream Big. Find Your Courage. Take Chances.

. . . . . . . . .

# DIANA NYAD

*"I started asking myself those basic existential questions, the poet Mary Oliver's incredibly penetrating look-in-the-mirror question: What is it you're doing with this one wild and precious life of yours? One day, it hit me like a ton of bricks. Cuba, that's what I'm going to do. Maybe I won't have the shoulders; maybe I won't have the will. Cuba for me was never about records. It was never about halls of fame. It wasn't about sport. It was about living large. It was about tapping every drop of potential that you have, physically, emotionally."*

. . . . . . . . . . . .

Diana was the first person to swim 111 miles from Cuba to Florida without the aid of a shark cage. She was sixty-four years old when she accomplished what she had tried but failed to do in her twenties. She is a longtime sports broadcaster, has written for *The New York Times*, NPR's "All Things Considered," and *Newsweek,* and is the author of four books, including: *Find a Way: The Inspiring Story of One Woman's Pursuit of a Lifelong Dream.*

# CHARLOTTE BEERS

*"One day you will need to know: What is the highest form of who you can be?*

*"It's not necessarily where you are today."*

## MARY WILSON

*"Whether you're dreaming about becoming a star, or a CEO, or the First Lady, or dreaming about getting out of an abusive marriage—whatever it is, you have got to dare to dream."*

## LINDA CLIATT-WAYMAN

*"Take each minute and visualize what awesome things can happen for you in your life. Take an hour each day to create new and exciting missions for your life. Every day think like an entrepreneur and simply take risks to explore those new ideas, even when you are afraid. And intertwined throughout every day of your life, make sure you become your own consistent cheerleader."*

## DR. JEN ARNOLD

*"When I finally decided that being a physician was my dream, I had to take the first step of initiation . . . I filled out the medical school applications, and I had to decide in my personal statement: Was I going to tell everyone that I was a little person? I didn't know if anyone else out there was a little person in medical school. I didn't know of any other little person doctors.*

*"So, I said, 'You know what? I'd rather they know when I walk into that interview who they're meeting and not be taken aback.' So, I put it all out there . . . I had one doctor sitting there telling*

me, 'How can you do this? How are you going to do that? How are you going to put a chest tube in a patient?' And I thought, 'Oh my gosh. I'm only a sophomore in college. I don't know.'

"But in reality, they didn't think that I could do it. They said, 'How, possibly, at three foot tall, are you going to be able to do that?' Well, my answer was, 'You know what? You're right. I may not be able to very easily or physically put in a chest tube in a six-foot-tall patient. But I don't want to become a trauma surgeon. I want to become a pediatrician. I think I can do that.'"

## BRENÉ BROWN

"I was raised in a family where it was very binary. You were either courageous or you were fearful. You were either brave or were afraid. And as I look back on my career and my life, I think that's a false choice. The one thing that I've learned about stepping into our power and daring greatly is that most of us are afraid and brave every day in the exact same moment. And we don't have to choose. That tension gives birth to our courage."

## NINA TASSLER

"The best antidote to fear is your curiosity, passion, and creativity."

# CARLY FIORINA

*"Courage is acting in spite of fear, and a leader's greatest job is to help people see the possibilities—possibilities that are so compelling that it helps people move beyond their fears and build a better future."*

# LISA NIEMI SWAYZE

*"Fearless. I love that word. It sounds just like how fearless should sound."*

# ANITA PERRY

*"It's been said many times before, but it's important to remember that living fearlessly is not the same as living without fear. Nobody lives without fear. Living fearlessly is about finding the strength, the courage, to keep the fears we all have from controlling our lives.*

*"It's about having the determination to do the right thing for ourselves, our families, our communities, and our nation.*

*"It's about finding the confidence within ourselves to face and overcome the limits that are placed upon us from without and from within."*

Anita was the longest-serving First Lady of Texas and host of the Texas Conference for Women from 2000 to 2015. She was previously the director of nursing at Haskell Memorial Hospital and spent more than seventeen years in the nursing profession. She is married to Rick Perry, who currently serves as US Secretary of Energy. She's a native Texan.

## NINA TASSLER

*"I have gone ahead despite the pounding in my heart that says, turn back. Embracing change and confronting fear serve me well."*

## BRENÉ BROWN

*"If I could go back and whisper in the ear of my twenty-something self, I would say, 'Being vulnerable, being real, and being open is scary. It feels dangerous, and it feels unsafe. But it does not feel anywhere as dangerous or scary or as unsafe as standing on the outside of your life looking in, wondering what if I would have shown up? What if I would have said "I love you" first? What if I would have taken the promotion without knowing if I could do the job? What if I would have walked into my boss's office and said, "Look, I know everyone's super excited about this. I have big questions about the direction we're taking with this project."' I think to spend our lives on the outside looking in is the fastest way to grief and resentment."*

# NINA SHAW

*"You have to find that thing that makes you brave."*

. . . . . . . . . . . .

Nina is a talent lawyer and co-founder of Time's Up, an initiative dedicated to fighting systemic sexual harassment in entertainment and blue-collar workplaces. Nina has a long-standing commitment to the education of children and is an advocate for the education of girls and women. A *New York Times* article called her "The Hollywood Power Behind Those Seeking a Voice."

# LISA NIEMI SWAYZE

*"Fear is not something you can conquer. You can confront it.*

*"And it's how you do that on a daily basis that shows you what you're made of."*

# DIANA NYAD

*"You look at a star. Your dream is a shining star, way up there, and then you tuck that away, and you put in discipline, and you put in focus, and one day, months and years later, you may not be able to touch that final vision star of yours, but you'll be up there in the rarefied heavens, and it will be all worthwhile."*

# NANCY BRINKER

*"Each of us, in our own lives, in our own way, is challenged to be brave enough. Brave enough to find the passion that gives our hearts fulfillment, our souls purpose, and our lives meaning— whether raising the public consciousness or raising a family.*

*"Brave enough to dream big—at home or at work—and to pursue goals and visions that to others may seem impossible. Brave enough to believe that within each of us lies the power to make a difference by standing up, by speaking out, in our communities and in our country. Brave enough to persevere no matter how long it takes or how many times we fall.*

*"To persist and prevail in the face of overwhelming odds. And brave enough to never stop forgetting a simple truth: that by leading from the heart, by touching someone else's heart, we can truly change the world."*

. . . . . . . . . . . .

Nancy is the founder of Susan G. Komen, the world's largest nonprofit source of funding in the fight against breast cancer. In 1980, Nancy promised her dying sister, Susan, that she would do everything in her power to end breast cancer forever. She is the author of *Promise Me: How a Sister's Love Launched the Global Movement to End Breast Cancer* and other books. *Time* magazine named her to the list of the 100 most influential people in the world in 2008. She lives in Texas.

# MEG WHITMAN

*"I called my husband after I went out for the interview [as CEO of eBay] and I said, 'Hon, I think we should move to California.' And he was just a great supporter. I said, 'You know, it's kind of risky. It might not work out.' And what he said was, 'The worst thing that can happen is you get another job.' So, I think risk-taking is something that everyone should think about at all stages of their life. And obviously you have to take into account your family situation. But I've never been disappointed by sort of taking a leap into the unknown."*

. . . . . . . . . . . .

Meg is the former CEO and President of Hewlett-Packard Enterprise, and the former President and CEO of eBay, where she oversaw growth in annual revenue from $5.7 million to $8 billion. The author of *The Power of Many: Values for Success in Business and in Life,* she is currently the CEO of Quibi, a new short-form video platform.

# SOLEDAD O'BRIEN

*"Risky career decisions, frankly, are never about your career. They're always about the kind of life you want to lead and the kind of impact you want to have. And when you look at it through that lens, they're really not risky career decisions.*

*"A woman said to me today, in one of the hallways, 'Well, you know, but I feel lost. I'm not sure where I'm going.' And I would argue that feeling lost isn't being lost. You're not lost; you know one thing, that where you are is not really where you want to be. And that is not a small insight. You can take that and start creating a path that you want to be on."*

. . . . . . . . . . . .

Soledad is a broadcast journalist and producer and CEO of Starfish Media Group, a multi-platform media production company she founded. O'Brien co-anchored CNN's *American Morning* and anchored CNN's morning news program *Starting Point*. She is co-founder and board chairperson of the PowHERful Foundation, and co-author of *The Next Big Story: My Journey Through the Land of Possibilities*.

# SOLEDAD O'BRIEN

*"Taking chances isn't risk. It really is answering an opportunity and deciding you're going to do it."*

## BRENÉ BROWN

*"How many of you would be willing to parachute out of a plane for fun if they don't teach you how to land until you're in the air? NO! I want the lesson upfront on how to land. I don't want someone screaming out of the plane, 'When you get down there, tuck and roll.' That's too late. Here's the thing: If we don't know how to land, we will do anything to avoid falling. We've got to teach people how to land. If you don't have a culture that tolerates vulnerability and failure, do not ask people to innovate. There is no innovation, there is no creativity, without failure."*

## NINA SHAW

*"If you don't ask, you're not going to get. If you do ask, the worst that anyone can say is no and, because you asked, there's a chance they'll say yes."*

## SARA MARTINEZ TUCKER

*"My life's dream is to make sure every Hispanic child in America has a choice in creating their destiny . . . I had an opportunity to visit the Lilly Endowment in Indiana. And they had asked me, 'What will it take to do the work that you need to do?' And so I built a three-hour presentation, I pitched my case, and at the*

end they asked me, 'Did you put a price tag to this?' . . . I had [already prepared] a $10-million budget, a $25-million budget, and a $50-million budget.

"And on the plane ride, I kept stewing: Do I ask them to help me double in size? Do I ask them to help me increase my capacity five times? Do I ask them to increase my capacity 10 times? . . . After they asked me about the price tag, I walked to my briefcase [where] I had those three viewgraphs, and it was so easy for me to sit back and say, 'What would my kids want me to do?' So, I plopped the $50-million proposal on the table, and we got the $50 million dollars from them. I didn't walk in assuming that I ran a $5-million organization. I walked in assuming that my children needed me to be a $500-million organization, and $50 million was just a drop in the bucket."

## LINDA CLIATT-WAYMAN

"Aim high, because not taking a risk will only lead to regret."

## BRENÉ BROWN

"My words to you are the same thing that I say to myself when I wake up every morning: 'Go out, be courageous.' Own our stories, love each other, and really be grateful for the people in our lives who love us—not despite our imperfections and our *vulnerabilities—but love us because of our imperfections and our vulnerabilities. Because those are the people who matter. They're the people who are on the outside of the arena, who when things don't go well say, 'Yeah, that was hard, and it didn't work out. But you were brave.'"*

# 7

# Give Yourself Permission to Focus on Happiness

. . . . . . . . .

# SHERYL SANDBERG

"I remember about four months after I lost [my husband] Dave, I was at a family party and a high school friend dragged me onto the dance floor, and I danced. And then, I literally burst into tears and had to be taken out. It was super embarrassing. I couldn't figure out exactly what was wrong because I had been grieving and crying a lot. But this felt different. Then I realized, I felt happy—for one moment, literally, maybe 30 seconds on a dance floor. And the guilt just flooded into my body. Like, 'What am I doing on a dance floor when Dave's not here and will never dance again?'

"Right around that time, my brother-in-law called me. He had only one brother, and he lost Dave, too. And he said, 'All Dave ever wanted was for you and your children to be happy. Don't take that away from him in death.'

"What I needed was permission to feel joy, permission because it's not just the loss, and it's not just the struggle. It's the guilt survivors feel, whether we were involved or not. And let's be clear: People make mistakes, and there are tragedies that stem from mistakes, and people need to be forgiven for those, too. But the guilt that we have moving on and finding joy is so real. I needed to be given permission not to feel that."

. . . . . . . . . . . .

Sheryl is an executive, author, and activist, and is the Chief Operating Officer at Facebook and the Founder of Leanin.org. She is co-author with Adam Grant of *Option B: Facing Adversity, Building Resilience, and Finding Joy.* She was once an aerobics instructor.

# ISABEL ALLENDE

"It's embarrassing for a woman especially, to admit that one is joyful. It means that one is not paying attention. One has no understanding or empathy for the state of the world. It's sinful to abandon oneself in the simple pleasure of being in the body and doing those things that are fun. However, joy and pleasure are essential in nature. Without the joy of color and fragrance of flowers, bees would not pollinate. Without the pleasure of sex, none of us would be here, because the only reason to do something so silly as intercourse is that it feels really nice. Joy is the force that moves nature."

# GRETCHEN RUBIN

"Happiness has a surprisingly bad reputation. Some people assume that happy people are stupid, or smug, or superficial. In fact, research shows—and I think you'll really see this borne out by your own experience—happy people are more interested in the people around them and more interested in the problems of the world. They're more altruistic. They give away more money. They volunteer more time. They're more likely to help out if a friend, family member, or colleague needs a hand. They're healthier, and they have healthier habits. They make better team members and better leaders. When we're unhappy, we tend to become isolated, defensive, and preoccupied with our own problems. When we're happy, we have the emotional wherewithal to turn outward. So, if it is selfish to want to be happy, we should be selfish—if only for selfless reasons."

## SHERYL SANDBERG

"I think when we think of happiness or joy, we often think of the big things in life. We're going to get married, we're going to get a job, we're going to have a child, someone's going to graduate. And those moments are joyful. But, really, joy is the small everyday stuff. And paying attention to those things makes a really big difference."

## ISABEL ALLENDE

"One can choose to nurture love, or let it dry up in the sands of everyday inconveniences. Abundance of love—that's the key to joy."

## SHAWN ACHOR

"We know happiness is an advantage. We know happiness is contagious. What we recently realized is happiness can't be a self-help pursuit. We have to do it with other people."

## GRETCHEN RUBIN

"Ancient philosophers and contemporary scientists agree that the key to a happy life is strong relationships with other people. To be happy, we have to have enduring, intimate relationships. We need to be able to confide. We need to feel like we belong. We need to be able to get support, and—just as important for happiness—give support. So, any time you're thinking about how to spend your precious time, energy, or money, something that deepens your existing relationships or broadens your existing relationships is something that's very likely to make you happier."

## ISABEL ALLENDE

"In joy, everything blossoms: creativity, truth, energy, love, compassion, strength."

## SHERYL SANDBERG

"Adam Grant told me to write down three moments of joy before I go to bed. And this is something I'm still doing in a little notebook, and they can be small: My daughter gave me a hug without being asked—hinted at, but not directly asked; my coffee tasted great this morning, even though I am currently trying to cut down to just two cups on doctor's orders. And I realized that before this suggestion, I went to bed every single night worried *about what I did wrong before [my husband] Dave died and then worried about the loss when Dave died. And it doesn't take all that away, but just giving myself the moment to focus on joy makes a big difference. It also makes a difference throughout the day, because when I get to see Adam, when my parents are here, and I get to give them a hug, I notice: 'This is joy, and this will make the notebook.' So it makes me more cognizant of and focused on these moments all day. No matter what you've been through, try it. Three moments of joy can make a big difference."*

## ISABEL ALLENDE

*"At my age, I need to have fun. I have no time for pessimism and gloom, and I hope you don't either."*

# 8

# Grow from Challenges. Surpass Limitations.

. . . . . . . .

# ANN RICHARDS

*"When you do the daily things of your life that are wearing you down and you think, 'I cannot make it,' continue to hold fast, hold your head up, be who you are—and you will collide with your destiny."*

. . . . . . . . . . . .

Ann was the forty-fifth Governor of Texas and known for her feminism, wit, and one-liners. She first came to national attention as a keynote speaker at the 1988 Democratic National Convention. In 1990, she successfully ran for governor—with a promise to increase the role of women and minorities in state government. She is the author of two memoirs, *Straight from the Heart* and *I'm Not Slowing Down.* At the time of her death in September 2006, Richards was actively involved in planning the Ann Richards School for Young Women Leaders in Austin. Ann was a huge supporter of the Conferences for Women and was instrumental in the launch of the Pennsylvania Conference for Women.

# JODY CONRADT

*"I don't believe people really find out what they are about or what they are capable of until they face adversity."*

. . . . . . . . . . . .

With 900 career victories, Jody is one of the winningest coaches in women's college basketball history. Former head coach of the

University of Texas women's basketball team, she is an inductee in the Texas Women's Hall of Fame. She's a native Texan.

## ABBY WAMBACH

*"Too often nowadays we're predisposed to talk about the things we're good at, the things we succeeded at. Really the thing I learned the most from was the first heartbreak in my life. I think that when we think about our life, [we focus] on the big spectrum. But when you're on your deathbed, not to be too morbid, you're going to think about the [smaller] things that you worked through and you overcame."*

## SOLEDAD O'BRIEN

*"A safe and easy path through life is not going to get you where you want to be. You have to be tested and then rise to that challenge, and fall, and rise, and fall, to get to where you want to be."*

## JENNY LAWSON

*"The horrible, terrible moments in our life, the ones that we want to forget ever happened, the ones that we want to pretend never happened, those are the moments that make us us. We should embrace them and celebrate them, and say: 'I'm weird and*

*flawed and messed up, but in the best possible way. Nobody is messed up like I'm messed up.' And be proud of that, and a little ashamed, but then more proud."*

. . . . . . . . . . . .

A self-described "professional weirdo," Jenny is a journalist, author, and blogger who is known as The Bloggess. She is the *New York Times* best-selling author of *Let's Pretend This Never Happened (A Mostly True Memoir)* and the more recent *You Are Here: An Owner's Manual for Dangerous Minds.* And, she is a Texan.

## BERTICE BERRY

*"I have learned that obstacles come to change me so that I am ready for the next leg of life."*

. . . . . . . . . . . .

Bertice is a sociologist, lecturer, educator, stand-up comedian, and talk-show host. She is the author of *Walking with Purpose, Colliding with Destiny: An Instructional Pathway to Purposeful Living,* two memoirs, several novels, and other books. Despite being told to give up on college, she holds a BA, an MA, and a PhD.

## CANDY CHANG

*"What you might consider your weaknesses can become your strengths. Being an introvert in an urban-planning world where*

the loudmouths ruled made me wonder how it could be different and more inclusive. My experiences with loss and depression and general confusion have often been the fire for my urban experiments. So be sensitive to your struggles and your shortcomings and the times that you feel out of place—because if you take the time to understand them, you might find an opportunity to change the system."

## CARLY FIORINA

"When I came to Hewlett-Packard, I was famously quoted as saying the glass ceiling doesn't exist. I didn't mean that I didn't understand bias or prejudice or the burdens that people who are different, and women in particular, carry. I understand them well. I have felt them all. What I meant is that nothing should stop a woman from achieving the life that she chooses."

## KATHLEEN DAELEMANS

"I got rejected a lot, but every no is a step closer to a yes. Every no is an opportunity to refine your pitch, and you've just got to bounce back. I'd give myself fifteen minutes to pout and that's it; fifteen minutes and we've got to move on. It's a busy day, and a lot of people have it a lot worse."

# LEYMAH GBOWEE

*"When you decide that this power that you have is possible, you always have a group of people out there telling you it's not possible. I tell young people all the time: Look at great men and women. When they start doing things, everyone thinks [they're] crazy. I'm sure when they were inventing Facebook everyone was laughing at those young people and saying, 'Facebook, that's the craziest idea.' Mandela spent 27 years in prison; everyone thought he would die and never be a hero. Dr. King started his civil rights movement, a movement where black and white would sit together and everyone would be equal—as the Constitution of this great country says. Gandhi said Indians would go and do something, and they all were laughed at, scorned."*

# NANCY GILES

*"You never know what's going to happen down the line. You never know if the dream job that you think you want actually will still be that dream job a few years from now. Dreams can change, ideas can change, and they will. Being fired can be a gift; things falling apart can be a strange kind of a release."*

. . . . . . . . . . . .

Nancy is an actress, commentator, and self-described "accidental pundette." She is writer and contributor to *CBS Sunday Morning*. She starred in *China Beach* and *Delta*, and has had guest roles in several other TV shows, including *Law & Order*.

For more than twenty years, she has helped at-risk kids take part in classes, performances, and acting, playwriting, and poetry workshops.

## LISA NIEMI SWAYZE

*"So often we push up against things, and they push right back. Whereas, when we stand in our truth, our intention, our bliss, the obstacles seem to melt away."*

## SOLEDAD O'BRIEN

*"I had a terrible secret and awful handicap called children. I don't know if any of you have heard of that awful disease: It drags you down, sometimes makes you tired, worn out. And I remember at NBC, I pitched a story, when Camp X-Ray was being built in Guantanamo, to go cover the first prisoners that were being held at Camp X-Ray. And they loved the story, and they loved it so much (I was eight months pregnant with my second child, a daughter) that they gave it to a colleague of mine, who was not eight months pregnant with his second child. And so, I did what any self-respecting, water-retaining, pissed-off pregnant woman would do, which was pitch a fit until someone put me on a plane to cover my own story."*

## DR. JEN ARNOLD

*"Yes, I have limitations. I'm three feet tall. Everybody has limitations."*

## SHERYL SANDBERG

*"One of the early things Adam [Grant] said to me was: 'Things could be worse.' He's the best professor at Wharton. I thought the guy was really smart. My husband died suddenly, and he's like, 'Things could be a lot worse and you should think about that.' I just looked at him like, 'What do you mean?' And he said, 'Dave could have died of that same cardiac arrhythmia driving your children.' And in one moment I was like, 'Oh my God, I'm lucky . . .'*

*"It's so counterintuitive when you're going through something horrible to think about even worse thoughts. You kind of think I should be looking for the positive. But reminding ourselves of gratitude is so important . . ."*

## BERTICE BERRY

*"Don't let the little things keep you from doing the big ones."*

## SHERYL SANDBERG

*"I turned forty-eight in August, and that's the birthday Dave never had. And before Dave died, I would have woken up that morning being like, 'Oh my God, I'm almost 50. Were those hot flashes that are happening to me at night?' And I woke up that morning with a very deep, profound sense of: 'I made it. I'm 48.'"*

## SOLEDAD O'BRIEN

*"There will always be someone there trying to talk you out of what you're doing. Plow on anyway."*

## JESSICA DILULLO HERRIN

*"Every day, you can wake up in the morning and make a choice—to live a more bold and joyful life. It is a choice. You have to choose to ignore the naysayers, to pursue a passion, to be daring, to be different, to be kind, to be open to what the universe has to give you. You have to choose to be fearlessly resilient."*

. . . . . . . . . . . .

Jessica is the CEO and founder of Stella & Dot Family Brands and the *Wall Street Journal* best-selling author of *Find Your Extraordinary: Dream Bigger, Live Happier, and Achieve*

*Success on Your Own Terms.* She was included on *Inc.*'s list of Top Ten Female CEOs in 2012. She has rock climbed in Thailand, gone diving in Egypt, and lived in Austin, Texas.

# SHERYL SANDBERG

*"Resilience is not just a muscle we build in ourselves; this is about being there for others. It's a muscle we build in each other. We build it in our children as parents. We build it in our parents as children. We build it in our communities, in our schools, in our companies and our organizations, and in our country. And it's something that, boy, we need a lot of right now."*

# 9

# Help, Thoughtfully

# ADAM GRANT

*"I want to create a world where givers succeed—where, instead of people being afraid that others are out to get them and being paranoid, they actually feel a state of paranoia, which is the delusional belief that other people are plotting your well-being, going around behind your back and saying exceptionally nice things about you."*

# MELINDA GATES

*"More than eleven years ago now, when I was engaged to Bill, and my wedding day was approaching, a bridal event was held in my honor. It was a small gathering of only women present, mostly friends and family members. They offered short talks and toasts. One of the women who spoke was Bill's mother, Mary Gates. She read aloud from a wonderful letter about marriage that she'd written to me, and at the close, she said, 'For those to whom much is given, much is expected.' At the time of our wedding, Mary was seriously ill with cancer, and she was sending me a message that was tender and affectionate, but also deeply serious. Mary and her husband, Bill Sr., had always done wonderful things with their own charitable giving. She wanted to make sure that her son and I did the same, and yet so much more."*

. . . . . . . . . . .

Melinda is a philanthropist and co-chair and co-founder of the Bill & Melinda Gates Foundation, the largest private charitable organization in the world. She is the author of the 2019 book, *The Moment of Lift: How Empowering Women Changes the World*. Her first job was tutoring children in math and computer programming. She was born and raised in Dallas.

# BERT JACOBS

*"We're helping kids with social and emotional wellness. We're helping kids to be optimists—kids who live in the worst neighborhoods, kids who face violence, kids who are facing diseases . . . They sometimes are so struck with trauma that they forget to be kids. We're empowering them to be kids again and someday to be leaders. How do we do it? Why do we do it? We do it because it feels good. What we've learned through the years is it will help your business, and it's smarter money spent in advertising. It's where capitalism is going. Capitalism is starting to solve more and more social issues."*

. . . . . . . . . . . .

Bert is the co-founder and Chief Executive Optimist of the Life is Good Company, an American apparel and accessories wholesaler, retailer, and lifestyle brand. A one-time ski instructor and pizza delivery guy, he teamed up with his brother to sell T-shirts on the streets of Boston—which ultimately led to a $100-million business that donates 10% of its profits to the Life is Good Kids Foundation. He's the co-author of *Life Is Good*.

# LEIGH ANNE TUOHY

*"Learn the power of cheerful giving . . . We really believe that the person who puts five bucks in the Salvation Army bucket at Christmas with a happy heart is going to reap more benefits than the person that writes a $10,000 check to Haiti because his publicist told him to do it. We're all capable of getting involved and making a difference."*

# SHERYL WUDUNN

*"When scientists have looked at the brain and what happens when we give, they find out that it stimulates a pleasure center that is the same area of the brain that is stimulated when we eat chocolate chip cookies and ice cream, when we flirt, fall in love, have sex. It is that pleasure center of the brain. And in fact, in half or more subjects that they've analyzed, it turns out that those people feel more intense pleasure when they give than when they receive. And, so, you actually can feel happier when you give. Neuroscience has proven what the Bible has said for hundreds of centuries."*

. . . . . . . . . . . .

Sheryl won the Pulitzer Prize with her husband, Nicholas Kristof, for their coverage of the Tiananmen Square protests of 1989 while correspondents for *The New York Times*. She has co-authored four best sellers with Kristof, including *Half the Sky:*

*Turning Oppression into Opportunity for Women Worldwide.* She was a former Vice President at Goldman Sachs and is currently Senior Managing Director at Mid-Market Securities, LLC.

## LINDA CLIATT-WAYMAN

*"While you are taking the steps to get to that place where you really want to be in your life, don't periodically glance back. Turn all the way around, and take time to help those who you passed on your journey to success—those people that in some small or big way helped you find your way."*

## PAT MITCHELL

*"For those of us who've made it through the glass ceiling, let's worry less about that now, and more about dropping ladders down for the women who come behind us."*

. . . . . . . . . . . .

Pat was the first woman president of PBS and CNN Productions. She is an award-winning TV and film producer and the co-curator and host of TEDWomen, an annual global conference. Author of the 2019 book *Becoming a Dangerous Woman: Embracing Risk to Change the World,* she places special importance on voices and stories of women in the media.

# RACHAEL RAY

*"Don't be afraid of hard work, and if you have great business skills, use them to build for your community too. You can really build great models for the way you give back. You can build that exponentially."*

. . . . . . . . . . . .

Rachael is a businesswoman, celebrity chef, and Food Network TV personality. She is the founder and editorial director of *Every Day with Rachael Ray* magazine and the author of *Everyone Is Italian on Sunday*. The winner of three Daytime Emmy Awards, she hosts the show *Rachael Ray* and three other Food Network series. She was once a waitress at Howard Johnson's and a candy counter at Macy's Marketplace. She loves Austin, Texas, for its music.

# MARION JONES

*"I learned that life is not about sport. Sport is not about life. Life is about how you can give back, how you can help people live a better life, how you can help people make better choices in their own lives."*

. . . . . . . . . . . .

Marion was the first woman to win five track-and-field medals at a single Olympics, but later returned the medals after admitting to having used performance-enhancing drugs. She served six months in prison for lying to federal investigators and now uses her story to encourage young people to do the right thing. She's the author of *On the Right Track: From Olympic Downfall to Finding Forgiveness and the Strength to Overcome and Succeed.* She has lived in Texas.

# ADAM GRANT

*"It's critical to be thoughtful about how you help. One of the biggest mistakes we see givers make is [to] try to help in every possible way. And then, they get a reputation for being nice people, and soon no good deed goes unpunished. What works much better is to develop a reputation as someone with specific skills or a core area of expertise who's willing to help in a particular area.*

*"I would encourage you to think about, 'What are those two or three forms of giving that you enjoy and excel at that can be done as five-minute favors?' And then, when people ask you for help in other ways, offer instead, 'Look, these are my real areas of expertise. If I can contribute in one of these ways, please let me know.' And, then your reputation changes because you get to be proactive about giving, as opposed to reactive. You do it on your own terms in the ways that add the most value.*

*"If you can align the giving that you do with the learning that you want to do, that actually contributes to your success."*

## SHERYL SANDBERG

*"I used to get this wrong all the time. If anyone was going through anything, I would say, 'Is there anything I can do?' And I meant it really sincerely. But on the other side of that question, what do you say? 'Well, can you make Father's Day disappear so I don't have to live through it every year?' Rather than offering to 'do anything,' do something."*

## SOLEDAD O'BRIEN

The following is a story Soledad shared after hearing it from missionaries in Haiti.

*"A boy is walking along the beach, and the tide's gone out. And there are starfish that are beached on the sand. So, the kid starts picking up starfish and throwing them back in the water, one by one. And a man comes up to him and says, 'What are you doing? This beach goes on for miles; there are literally a million starfish on the beach. This is a waste of your time.' And the kid picks up a starfish and says, 'Well, I guess it matters to this one,' and chucks it back in."*

## LEYMAH GBOWEE

*"I've been to many places, and I've seen many women. And I've seen work that great women do. But you know what? It doesn't*

*take a lot, it doesn't take a whole budget, and it doesn't take proj-ect proposals. Sometimes it takes nothing at all but just a simple smile or a hug or a pat on the shoulder to say, 'You can make it, and I know you can.'"*

## SOLEDAD O'BRIEN

*"We, as women, are notoriously terrible about asking for help, and I might be the terriblest. But an executive who finally insisted that I should rely on her help as a CEO, in her own transition, said, 'You know, me helping you, Soledad, helps me.'*

*"There are people who want to help. Find them and sit with them, and network with them, and strategize with them, and ask, and ask, and ask."*

## RUTH SIMMONS

*"People make much of the fact that I'm the first black president of an Ivy League university. I'll tell you what I'm proud of: I'm proud of the fact that a mother and father struggled long and hard to raise a family and that I took advantage of everything they had to offer me. I'm delighted that they paved the way for me, and I want to work to pave the way for others. I hope that somewhere in your success, you keep a little space to look back for the people who need you to pave the way for them."*

# SHERYL WUDUNN

*"If you just have an open heart, an open mind, you can really transform someone else's life. And after all, isn't that what we're all here for?"*

# 10

# Lead Like the Women We Need

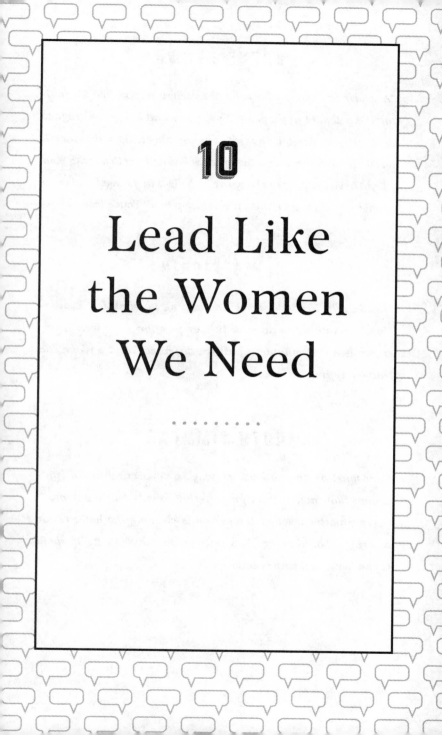

# BRENÉ BROWN

"A leader is anyone who holds themselves responsible for finding the potential in people and processes and has the courage to develop that potential. That's it. It has nothing to do with salary; it has nothing to do with the big office; it has nothing to do with your title. Are you willing to show up and believe in yourself and other people and work your butt off to develop that? That's leadership."

# CARLY FIORINA

"Leadership is about seeing and seizing possibilities. Leadership has nothing to do with title or position or power. Leadership is about making a positive difference; and anyone can lead—anytime, anywhere."

# RUTH SIMMONS

"You must be able to lead the way in advocating broad leadership; that makes room for differing talents and opinions. It doesn't matter whether the person is cleaning the hallways or chairing a board of directors meeting. Talent is talent. Goodwill is goodwill. Capacity is capacity."

# CARLY FIORINA

*"I know beyond the shadow of a doubt that leaders are made, not born."*

# JOHNITA JONES

*"I believe that women are effective leaders when they are very clear communicators. You can't mince words. You have to call it like you see it. And you need to be assertive. Guys get places by being assertive and saying what they want. Women need to understand that it's OK for them to do that also."*

. . . . . . . . . . . .

Johnita served as President of the Texas Conference for Women board for more than a decade. She is also Vice President / Southern Operations Manager at ExxonMobil Pipeline Company. She has also served on the Advisory Board of the Houston Children's Museum and on the board of directors of the Lighthouse of Houston.

# BRENÉ BROWN

*"Courageous leaders are never silent about hard things. That's what differentiates leaders from other people. Leaders say, 'I'm going to excavate and bring to the surface and shine a light on the stuff that we're all feeling but no one's talking about.' That's*

leadership. And it's hard. And it's brave. And you're going to mess up. But you're going to feel alive and brave and proud of who you are, even as they're handing you an ass-kicking. Because those really tough moments are when we feel the most sure that we've done the right thing."

## CHARLOTTE BEERS

"No one ever leads without learning to speak clearly, memorably, and going overtly for persuasion. This is harder for us women. We would like to let the facts speak for us—like 'The report indicates . . .' It's particularly difficult if you're in the sophisticated tech world, because you can prove a lot of things, but the things that matter, that influence, persuade, and move people are never provable.

"What are you going to use? You're going to use your ability to believe, to be so articulate, to be in such a center of what you need to have happen that you turn around and people are following you. That is called leadership. How do you get there? You practice it every single day."

## BRENÉ BROWN

"We found 150 leaders across the world—from Pixar to the CIA, from special forces to civic and political leaders—and we asked one question: What does the future of leadership look like?

*Who is going to be standing in five years, and who will be gone? Because we have huge problems to solve . . . and an insatiable need for more innovation . . .*

*"Everyone said the same thing: We have to have braver leaders. We have to have more courageous cultures. We need more bold people to lead."*

## RUTH SIMMONS

*"We need to have communities of leadership that go beyond the CEO and the senior vice presidents of an organization. We need to have an understanding of how important it is to say to an organization that no one group, no one individual, can sustain the health of an organization over time and constant change. The best model validates every person, every level of authority, every person's talents, and I think we've got to move quickly to that model.*

*"I think women happen to be very good at leadership because they have been educated to share power, to acknowledge others' accomplishments, to give others credit for what they've done, to fight for the visibility of the unseen colleague, and to collaborate with—rather than merely compete."*

## LEYMAH GBOWEE

*"When my sisters and I banded together and decided that we would take on one of the most brutal warlords in the history of*

*Africa, they called us toothless bulldogs, a bunch of old married women looking for press or public attention . . . all kinds of names. Today we are in the history books because we knew that we had to do something."*

# 11

# Make Good Choices and Own Your Influence

. . . . . . . . . .

# ANITA HILL

*"Media pundits predicted that no woman would ever come forward after witnessing the treatment that I received [in the 1991 Clarence Thomas hearings]. There would be no more sexual harassment complaints filed. Now we know that the media pundits were wrong. Women, in fact, came forward. But the pundits weren't just wrong about the numbers. The pundits were wrong because they underestimated the will of women to stop the abuses that they had experienced. And that is what we have to keep in mind—that you may get messages to tell you that you are weak, or you are powerless, or you are not brave enough to come forward. But we know better. We know that we can tap into our own power and our own sense of what is right and wrong, to step up, to make a difference in our lives, in the lives of people who we care about, and all women."*

. . . . . . . . . . . .

Anita is a lawyer and professor of social policy, law, and women's studies at Brandeis University, who became a national figure in 1991 when she testified against Clarence Thomas, then a Supreme Court nominee—accusing him of sexual harassment while he was her supervisor at the United States Department of Education and the Equal Employment Opportunity Commission. She is the author of an autobiography, *Speaking Truth to Power, and Reimagining Equality: Stories of Gender, Race, and Finding Home.*

## CARLY FIORINA

*"We cannot always choose our circumstances, but we can always choose our response to those circumstances."*

## MARION JONES

*"As women, our choices and actions shape the future in powerful ways—on our jobs, in our communities, and perhaps most importantly, in our homes and in our personal lives."*

## ISABEL ALLENDE

*"I have no time to hold grudges, buy expensive brands, or go on diets. My days, like your days, are counted, so I'm going to enjoy writing and reading novels, sleeping with my dog and my current lover (given that I can't sleep with my favorite movie actor), eating dark chocolate, and drinking red wine. I will be generous because it makes me feel really good. I'm going to wear lipstick, and keep myself in love. I will take pole-dancing lessons, and practice the best kind of love. Love, like joy, is a choice."*

## KATHLEEN DAELEMANS

*"I always had this instinct and this voice in my head that said, 'Follow your passion. Somehow, the money will follow.' It truly,*

*truly does. If you have no idea where to start, just listen to that*
*voice inside your head, and network, network, network."*

## CARLY FIORINA

*"I started out as a medieval history and philosophy major. That*
*means I was unemployable. And because I was unemployable,*
*I decided to do what my father wanted me to do. He was a law*
*professor. And he wanted me to go to law school and so I went*
*off to law school. And I discovered pretty quickly that I hated it.*
*So I made the first adult choice, certainly the first tough choice*
*of my young life at that time. I decided to go home and tell my*
*parents I quit. I wasn't a quitter. In fact, I was something of*
*an obnoxious Goody Two-shoes as a child. And they, of course,*
*responded in the way parents sometimes do when they said,*
*'Carly, we're very disappointed.'*

*"But I knew despite my parents' disappointment, that living*
*my life to please someone else was not a worthy goal. And I also*
*knew then that if I did not have passion for what I was going to*
*do, then I would never be successful at it."*

## MEG WHITMAN

*"The advice I give to young people all the time, and give to col-*
*leagues if they're thinking about changing careers or changing*

direction, is first and foremost: Do something that you absolutely love and are passionate about."

## KAREN HUGHES

"I always encourage young people to choose their bosses very carefully. And I say that not only because mine went on to become the President, but also because I've learned over my career that the example set by your boss—their priorities—can either support or undermine your own."

## SUZE ORMAN

"Are you becoming the powerful women you were born to be?"

## CHARLOTTE BEERS

"You can learn [how to be an artful communicator]. I had to learn it. Everybody I've ever met has had to go through that tunnel of learning on how to be more masterful in their communication. What does it sound like when you're being an artfully clear communicator? You're speaking with clarity, from the center of yourself; you're clear, you are speaking in a memorable way—because you've acquired the skills to do it. You're poetic, you're visual."

## SUZE ORMAN

*"Understand that if you could just connect to that power that is within you, if you could just do what was right versus what was easy, the end results would be your own greatness."*

## VIOLA DAVIS

*"That's your power as a woman. It's not in degrees. It is in your joy. It's in your nurturing, it's in your kids, but hell, it's also in your failures. It's in your shortcomings. It's in that extra 20 pounds of weight you have. Screw it. Be alive. Embrace it all."*

## MARTHA BECK

*"You might want to try a little experiment. Go into a Starbucks in a state of agitation, worried about a problem, and just watch how other people behave just like people always behave. Everyone's in a hurry. Everyone's scared. 'Oh, my gosh, I've got to get to work. I've spilled coffee. It's terrible. I may have to sell one of my homes.'*

*"Then go in the next day, but go in with your mind full of the thought, 'All is well.' Look around at other people and think, without speaking, 'May you be well, may you be happy. May you be free from suffering.' First of all, you'll start to feel more calm, confident, and comfortable.*

*"Secondly, other people will start behaving very oddly.*

*They'll smile more. They'll physically move toward you. They'll offer you gifts. The barista may give you something extra for free. I'm telling you, this is so cool. Just try it."*

. . . . . . . . . . . . .

Martha is one of the world's best-known life coaches, a Harvard-trained sociologist, and best-selling author. On that point, she has said: "I'm shocked every time someone introduces me as a 'best-selling author,' because I've never written to sell myself, only to save myself. Writing is my favorite tool for addressing and dis-solving my own suffering. At some point I discovered that it could help others, too." Her books include *Expecting Adam, Finding Your Own North Star,* and more. Oprah has described her as "one of the smartest women I know."

# 12

# Mothers
# and
# Other
# Mentors

. . . . . . . . .

# MELINDA GATES

"When I was in seventh grade at St. Monica Elementary School in Dallas, Texas, I had a very special teacher by the name of Sister Judith Marie. I didn't know I was good in math, but she did. She put me in an accelerated group with a bunch of boys—and me. I worked harder than I ever worked before, but it was thrilling. I realized that I loved math. So, when I went on to high school at Ursuline Academy, my teachers kept pushing me in math and encouraging me in my new passion, which became computers.

"One phenomenal woman, Mrs. Bower, my math teacher, managed through hard grit to get us 10 personal computers for our class. They were Apple IIs. At the time—this was in 1980— she was a single mom, working full-time, raising three boys, and getting her PhD in computer science on the side. But she wasn't going to let us miss out on computers. And you know what? She set me on my way."


# DIANA NYAD

"One day, I was standing with my French mother on the beach in Fort Lauderdale. I said, 'Mom, I know it's out there somewhere, but I can't see it. Where is Cuba?' She said, 'Okay, come here. I'm going to show you. Lift up your arm this way. No, this way more. There, it's right there. As a matter of fact, it is so close you could almost swim there.' That wasn't the start of a concrete dream but, I'll tell you, it was a little flutter in the back of the imagination."

# MEG WHITMAN

*"My mother is an intrepid innovator and really an intrepid woman of her generation. She's 88 years old, but did some amazing things with us as children, one of which was taking us on a three-month camping trip from Boston, Massachusetts, to Anchorage, Alaska, where we drove in a Ford Econoline van 3,000 miles across the unpaved Alcan Highway. It was my mom and my older brother and sister. We camped for three months, and my Dad joined us for his two-week vacation. It taught us resilience. It taught us connectivity. It taught us that there was great fun in being intrepid."*

# SARAH FERGUSON

*"My grandmother said, 'When in doubt or when you feel bad, go and give to someone.'"*

. . . . . . . . . . . .

In addition to being Duchess of York, Sarah, also known as "Fergie," is a writer, film producer, TV personality, and philanthropist. She is the founder of Children in Crisis, a nonprofit organization aimed at improving the lives of children and women from underprivileged backgrounds in third-world countries. She is also the author of *Finding Sarah: A Duchess's Journey to Find Herself.*

## ANNE-MARIE SLAUGHTER

*"My mother raised three successful children who are strong and have contributed to the economy and to society in different ways. She created a support structure. Without that family, I can't be here. I can't do what I do. They're my foundation. It's not that it's a tug of war: Family enables me to be the person I am. In the corporate world, we call it investment in human capital. As a society, that's the most important work we do."*

## SOLEDAD O'BRIEN

*"I used to ask my mom what it was like to be in Baltimore in the early 1960s with children, and she used to tell me: 'People would spit on us, as we would walk down the street together.'*

*"I said, 'Oh my goodness, what did you do?'*

*"And, she said: 'Oh, lovey, we knew America was better than that, and we could be part of making it better.' I thought this was the most amazing thing, and it framed for me a lot of how I think about the stories that I tell. It's that sense of optimism that I've always held on to, which is the American story—one of change and growth, and opportunities to be better."*

# BERT JACOBS

"The first person who inspired us, and the biggest inspiration for 'Life is Good,' is our mom, Joan. When we got the news that she had terminal lung cancer, that it was moving fast, and there wasn't much we could do, we went to Mom and said, 'Is there anything that you'd love to do?' She lived such an ordinary life. 'Would you like to go to Europe? Would you like to meet the President? We don't know the President, but we'll get the shit done, Mom.'

"She thought about it and said, 'No, I'm the happiest I've ever been. I'm scared of the cancer. But I just want to be here. I don't want to be in the hospital, and I want to be with your father and you kids and the little ones.'

"We drove back to the city, me and [my brother] JJ, and it bothered us. We talked about it all week. Your own mom's dying, you know it. You want to help her, but how can you help her if she doesn't let you?

"Then JJ figured it out. He called me and said, 'Mom loved with all her heart her whole life and now that she knows she's dying, she doesn't have to run around and make up for love she wishes she gave.' So the next morning I got in the car and drove out to see my mom. Of course, I took credit for the theory.

"I said, 'Mom, we figured it out.' She said, 'Oh, that's really sweet, but I did think of something. Not now while I'm alive, but after I go, I want you to throw me a really good party.' So we did. We threw her an incredible party with music and dancing and food, and we can only hope that it lived up to her one request.

"Today, I ask you the question, since that day will come for you and that day will come for me. When that day comes, will we have to run around and make up for love we wished we gave? Or will we sit back like my mom did with a big smile and say, 'Throw me a good party'?"

# 13

# On Curiosity and Truth Telling

. . . . . . . . . .

# CANDY CHANG

"*I aspire to have the openness of mind where the strength of a leaf can lead you to reimagine the way we build our buildings . . . I think that's the core of how good ideas develop. Following your curiosity. Experimenting and allowing your many life experiences to continue to influence you for the rest of your life.*"

# CARLY FIORINA

"*When I came into the room to be informed [that I had been fired], it turned out that all the board members had left. They weren't prepared to face me and tell me why they were doing what they were doing. In fact, I'm not even sure they knew, because they asked me to write the press release. They said, 'Why don't you say that this was your idea? That you've accomplished everything you set out to accomplish when you came here; say that you're ready to move on.' So I thought about that for a while and I said, 'No, the truth is you fired me.' And the truth is always the best answer, no matter what the consequences are.*"

# SALLIE KRAWCHECK

*"If it comes down to your job or your ethics, choose your ethics every time. You can always find another job. People often say, 'Look. But ethics are gray. This is okay. That is okay. When does it get not okay? How do you know?'*

*"And for all of us, I think we have to find out how we know. For me, it's my stomach. My stomach tells me every time. When I can't eat, something's wrong . . . Occasionally, my stomach lets me down.*

*"And, I don't know the answer to whether something crosses my line of ethics or not. And so, I have a very simple test, which is I ask what the person I would like to be would do—what the ideal version of myself would do. And I find I come to the right answer every single time. Simple exercise; important result."*

# ANONYMOUS
# (SHARED BY BRENÉ BROWN)

*"Clear is kind, unclear is unkind."*

# CANDY CHANG

*"The world becomes more rewarding when you let yourself look beyond what you're searching for. It's good to have goals, but it might be even greater to embrace serendipity and to allow random experiences to become meaningful to you and the other parts of your life. We can only have new insight into our working lives when we make ourselves available to it. When we're open and receptive to the unexpected."*

# CHRISTY HAUBEGGER

*"Do that crazy thing. Learn to rock climb. Learn to mountain bike. I learned to snowboard this year.*

*"I encourage you to learn and try new things because you just never know where the magic's going to strike you. I'm one of those people who would always rather think, 'Boy, I learned to do something—snowboarding—and I humiliated myself tremendously.'*

*"I'd so much rather remember that I tried something and failed miserably than to think I never tried and always wonder, 'What would that have been like?'"*

. . . . . . . . . . . .

Christy is the founder of *Latina* magazine, an agent with Creative Arts Agency, and a Stanford Law School graduate. *Advertising Age* named her a "Woman to Watch" and she is a member of the American Advertising Federation Hall of Achievement for her work in heightening awareness of the US Hispanic market. Her parents told her she could be whatever she wanted to be. She is a Texan.

*The Target Storyteller Winners*
*at the 2018 Texas Conference for Women.*

*Amal Clooney, a British human rights lawyer specializing in*
*international law. Her clients have included political prisoners, ousted*
*heads of state, and Nobel Peace Prize winner Nadia Murad.*

*Anita Hill, lawyer and professor of social policy, law, and women's studies at Brandeis University. She became a national figure in 1991 when she testified against then Supreme Court nominee, Clarence Thomas—accusing him of sexual harassment.*

*The Ann Richards School Band, which performed on the main stage at the 2018 Conference in front of a sold-out crowd of 7,500 attendees. The band represents the Ann Richards School for Young Women Leaders in Austin.*

*Melinda Gates, philanthropist and co-chair and co-founder of The Bill & Melinda Gates Foundation, the largest private charitable organization in the world. She is the author of the 2019 book,* The Moment of Lift: How Empowering Women Changes the World.

*Anne-Marie Slaughter, CEO of New America, former director of policy planning for the United States Department of State, and author of the highly influential* The Atlantic *article, "Why Women Still Can't Have It All."*

*Linda Cliatt Wayman, former principal of the Philadelphia's Strawberry Mansion High School, which was profiled for ABC World News Tonight and Nightline. Author of* Lead Fearlessly, Love Hard: Finding Your Purpose and Putting It to Work.

*Attendees participating in a breakout session on Mastering Civility in the Workplace at the 2017 Texas Conference for Women.*

*Laurie Dalton White, founder and executive director of the Conferences for Women.*

*Abby Wambach, soccer icon, two-time Olympic gold medalist, and winner of the 2015 FIFA Women's World Cup. She has scored more international goals than any woman or man in history. She is also the author of the 2019 book,* Wolfpack.

*Attendees participating in a breakout session at the*
*2016 Texas Conference for Women.*

*Brené Brown, research professor at the University of Houston*
*and an expert in courage, vulnerability, shame, and empathy. Author of four*
*#1 New York Times best sellers including, most recently,* Dare to Lead.

*Bert Jacobs, co-founder and Chief Executive Optimist of the Life is Good Company. He teamed up with his brother to sell T-shirts on the streets of Boston—which ultimately led to the creation of a $100-million business.*

*Mary Wilson, founding and longest serving member of the Supremes and former Cultural Ambassador for the U.S. State Department. Author of two best-selling memoirs and a forthcoming book,* Supreme Glamour.

*Attendees listening to Anita Hill during the opening keynote at the 2017 Texas Conference for Women.*

*Carly Fiorina, former CEO of Hewlett-Packard (HP) and the first woman to ever lead a Fortune 500 company. Former candidate for U.S. President, and author of* Find Your Way.

*Adam Grant, an organizational psychologist, Wharton School professor, and host of*
*WorkLife podcast. He is the author of* Originals: How Non-Conformists Move the
World *and co-author with Sheryl Sandberg of* Option B: Facing Adversity,
Building Resilience, and Finding Joy.

*Diana Nyad, the first person to swim 111 miles from Cuba to Florida without the aid*
*of a shark cage. She was sixty-four years old. A longtime sports broadcaster and the*
*author of four books, including* Find a Way.

*Attendees listening to singer Ruthie Foster during the luncheon keynote at the 2017 Texas Conference for Women.*

*Isabel Allende, novelist, feminist, philanthropist—and one of the most widely read authors in the world. She was inducted into the American Academy of Arts and Letters and awarded the 2014 Presidential Medal of Freedom.*

*Vernā Meyers, Vice President of Inclusion Strategy at Netflix, and founder of The Vernā Myers Company. Author of* What If I Say the Wrong Thing? 25 Habits for Culturally Effective People.

*Cathie Black, an angel investor, former President and Chairman of Hearst Magazines, and former President and Publisher of* USA Today. *She was the first woman publisher of a weekly consumer magazine,* New York Magazine.

*Shawn Achor, author and popular speaker known for his advocacy of positive psychology. Author of the* New York Times *best seller,* The Happiness Advantage, *and the 2018 book,* Big Potential.

*Viola Davis, actress, producer and the winner of the Academy Award, an Emmy, a Golden Globe, a Screen Actors Guild award, and a Tony Award. She is also the author of the children's book* Corduroy Takes a Bow.

*Charlotte Beers, former Chairman and CEO of Ogilvy & Mather Worldwide and former Undersecretary for Public Diplomacy and Public Affairs. She was the first woman to appear on the cover of* Fortune, *and is the author of* I'd Rather Be in Charge.

*Sheryl Sandberg, Chief Operating Officer at Facebook, Founder of Leanin.org, and co-author with Adam Grant of* Option B: Facing Adversity, Building Resilience, and Finding Joy.

*Attendees participating in a breakout session on Using Setbacks to Build Resilience at the 2017 Texas Conference for Women.*

*Leymah Gbowee, Nobel Peace Prize Laureate and the founder of the Gbowee Peace Foundation. She is Executive Director of the Women, Peace, and Security Program at Columbia University, and the author of* Mighty Be Our Powers.

*Participants of the Young Women's Program at the 2017 Texas Conference for Women.*

*Sheryl WuDunn, Pulitzer Prize-winning journalist and co-author with her husband, Nicholas Kristoff, of four best sellers, including* Half the Sky. *She is currently Senior Managing Director at Mid-Market Securities, LLC.*

*Candy Chang, artist, designer, urban planner— and a leader in participatory public art. She is the creator of the project, "Before I Die," a TED Senior Fellow, and was named a "Live Your Best Life" Local Hero by O, The Oprah Magazine.*

*Nina Shaw, talent lawyer and co-founder of Time's Up, an initiative dedicated to fighting sexual harassment. A New York Times article called her "The Hollywood Power Behind Those Seeking a Voice."*

*Sarah Ferguson* (middle), *Duchess of York, and a writer, film producer, TV personality, and philanthropist; Anita Perry* (right), *Texas First Lady and host of the Texas Conference for Women from 2000 to 2015.*

*Gretchen Rubin,* New York Times *best-selling author of* The Happiness Project *and, most recently,* Outer Order, Inner Calm: Declutter and Organize to Make More Room for Happiness.

*Johnita Jones, the President of the Texas Conference for Women board for more than a decade, and Vice President/Southern Operations Manager at ExxonMobil Pipeline Company.*

Left to right: *Laurie Dalton White, Founder and Executive Director; Amy Cooper, program director; and Gaye Polan, then Assistant Legislative Director for Governor Perry during the first Texas Conference for Women in 2000.*

# 14

# Progress:
# Past, Present,
# and Future

. . . . . . . . .

## ISABEL ALLENDE

*"When I think of the giant steps women have taken in my life-time, I'm very hopeful in spite of the huge task that lies ahead. The generation that started the women's liberation movement has aged gracefully. For the first time in history, there are millions of mature women empowered by education, work, and economic resources, who are healthy, energetic, and connected. We are benevolent witches. Our mission is to take care of young women, children, and the planet."*

## JESSICA DiLULLO HERRIN

*"Our grandmothers' generation sailed across oceans. They got the vote. They went to work when their country went to war. They clipped coupons, they raised families, they were resilient. We inherited that."*

## ABBY WAMBACH

*"I think where we're at now in our world is we need not just women, but men and women to stand up together to fight for all the right things that this world really truly does need. It's equal pay. It's equal opportunity. It's equal rights."*

# NINA SHAW

*"Over the forty years or so of your working lifetime, if you are making 70 cents on the dollar to your colleague, you will leave $1.4 million dollars on the table. You will take home less in the way of Social Security benefits because those benefits are calculated on your salary. You will be unable to afford to support yourself in your old age if you do not otherwise have someone who is contributing to your support. You will have less for your children. You will have less for your aging parents . . . So, I want you to think that when you fight for equal pay, you're fighting for what you are owed, but you are also fighting for your children, for your parents, for your security in old age, for your ability to start businesses."*

# JESSICA DILULLO HERRIN

*"Every day, I am inspired by watching the resilience of women adapting to changing circumstances and choosing to lead a more bold and joyful life, choosing to do less fretting and more doing, to do less wanting and more having."*

# ABBY WAMBACH

*"Wherever you are in your life, wherever you are in your career, learn from my mistakes. I was a little bit too scared to rock the*

*boat because I didn't want to lose my position. I didn't want to lose my spot on the team. I didn't want to lose any of that, because then I'd lose all the endorsements and all the money that comes in—because I have to pay my mortgage, and that's important.*

*"But what I lost was some time. I lost time to be able to mobilize not just my teammates, but mobilize women like you to do more work, because if I had worked two, three years ago, maybe we would be in a better place right now."*

## SHERYL SANDBERG

*"Every year is a gift."*

## CHRISTY HAUBEGGER

*"A few years ago, I went to Spain, and I remember seeing these enormous cathedrals that took 200 years to build. They didn't have bulldozers and all this equipment. And I thought to myself, 'What is it like if you're putting down the first stones in a cathedral knowing that you're never going to live to see your work done?' I feel like we are those women now. We're putting down the first stones in a cathedral. We are doing this for the next generation, for our daughters and our sons, and for all the women who are going to come behind us."*

# ISABEL ALLENDE

*"In the last few years, journalists keep asking me about passing the torch to younger women. I'm not dead yet. I have absolutely no intention of passing my torch. The embalmer will have to break it from my clutch. But I'm willing to light as many young women's torches as possible, and I will do it joyfully."*

# MEG WHITMAN

*"Our nation faces unprecedented challenges at home and abroad, and I believe we are at a defining moment for America, a moment when the decisions we make will set our country's destiny. And this is not a moment for anyone in this room to sit on the sidelines."*

# RUTH SIMMONS

*"My own formula for strong, diverse leadership among women focuses on the kind of education young women should receive, and what they will need to do to survive and lead in coming times. I always urge a woman [to] be demanding about her education. I say to women that they should not seek primarily to be validated as a learner; they need to feel challenged. That's how competence and growth flourish."*

# CHRISTY HAUBEGGER

*"I was on a really successful client call in Detroit. I'd gone to see Ford, and General Motors, and Chrysler. And I was staying in what's arguably the nicest hotel in Detroit. And when I'm coming back to my room, I went down the hall, got a bucket of ice, and I'm walking back to my room, wearing a charcoal pinstripe suit. This hotel guest walked out into the hallway, and she says, 'Oh, wonderful, dear. Are you bringing those to all the rooms?' And I said, 'No, ma'am, just my room.'*

*"Every time I hear something like that, every time that I've been tapped on the shoulder and asked to get coffee at a conference, it reminds me we're not done yet, because until that woman in the hallway sees me and thinks, 'You know what, I bet that's a publisher. I bet that's a lawyer'—until she thinks I'm as likely to be a hotel guest as a hotel domestic worker—we're not done yet."*

# RUTH SIMMONS

*"I come from a place that fear constructed, a place where people wanted to deny me the opportunity to be who I was, and who said to me all the way up through my young years, through my high school years, and all the way up through college, 'Ruth, you will never be able to do this, but if you're lucky and you work hard, you might be able to do this over here.'*

*"And I'm here to say that if you hold on, there's a wonderful thing about the world that God brought, and that is, it is turning,*

*and it is changing every day. If you do what you need to do, challenge yourself and be strong, eventually it's going to turn to where you are."*

# AMAL CLOONEY

*"Holding back women is holding back half of every country in the world and stifles progress for all of us. So, these are rights that we must all fight for."*

. . . . . . . . . . . .

Amal is a British human rights lawyer specializing in international law. Her clients have included political prisoners, ousted heads of state, and Nobel Peace Prize winner Nadia Murad. Together, Amal and Nadia took on ISIS, including at the United Nations.

# 15

# See the Possibilities

## SUZE ORMAN

*"None of you must ever forget that when one door closes, another one opens. None of you must ever forget every single 'No' leads you that much closer to a 'Yes.'"*

## CARLY FIORINA

*"There are people who focus on the limits, and there are people who focus on the possibilities. See the possibilities in whatever your circumstances are, and fill those possibilities. Run to the problem, not away from it, and opportunity will knock."*

## BERT JACOBS

*"Optimists see opportunities. They acknowledge the obstacles, but we focus on the opportunities, and we grow the opportunities. It's very simple."*

## SOLEDAD O'BRIEN

*"I think we need to think of our opportunities through the long view: What do we want to be working on ten years from now? What do we want to be remembered for if we were to drop dead tomorrow?"*

# LEYMAH GBOWEE

*"The power of possibility is the power that changes the world."*

# MALLIKA CHOPRA

*"There is a phrase from the Upanishads that says, 'You are what your deepest desire is. As is your desire, so is your intent. As is your intent, so is your will. As is your will, so is your deed. As is your deed, so is your destiny.'*

*"And so, sometimes we're struggling so hard to figure out our purpose and how we can contribute. But it just begins with knowing who we are and what our deepest desires are."*

. . . . . . . . . . . .

Mallika is a mother, author, businesswoman, entrepreneur, and meditation teacher. She is the author of *Living with Intent: My Somewhat Messy Journey to Purpose, Peace, and Joy* and *Just Breathe: Meditation, Mindfulness, Movement, and More.* She is co-founder of The Chopra Well with her brother, Gotham Chopra, and father, Deepak Chopra.

# LEYMAH GBOWEE

*"The power of possibility is only possible if you decide 'I'm going to step up and step out and do something.'"*

# 16

# Succeed

. . . . . . . . .

# CARLY FIORINA

*"Success, like leadership, is not about position. It is not about power. It is not about title. Success is about living a life that makes you happy and proud. Success is about making a positive difference for your community, for your family, for your company."*

# DR. JEN ARNOLD

*"I learned at a really early age that, if you wanted to do something, whether it be going to Disney World, or your dream is to climb Mount Everest, the first step of achieving that goal is just to try. You never know if you can do something until you at least give it a shot."*

# CATHIE BLACK

*"Getting ready for success is about taking the mountain by reaching your own summit. It's not enough, though, just to focus on the summit. You have to see the path that leads you there, a vision of your life and your road map for your own life. You must have clear direction. It means thinking that route through, including asking yourself, 'If I have to detour, what's the worst that can happen?' and preparing to answer that question."*

## SARA MARTINEZ TUCKER

*"I think that you have to find the intersection of your talents, your voice, and your heart, because when the three come together, you're able to be more effective."*

## DIANA NYAD

(At age twelve, in response to her father who worried that she was a fanatic because she practiced at four thirty a.m., her muscles were getting big, and her hair was green.)

*"Yes, I am a fanatic. That's how people get ahead in life. They're fanatics."*

## CATHIE BLACK

*"Women ask me all the time, 'How do you get ready and tough for success?' I do know about tough, after many decades in the business, and I know something about people in powerful positions, including those that I've worked with or for—Rupert Murdoch; Al Neuharth, the founder of USA Today; Oprah Winfrey; Gloria Steinem; Francis Ford Coppola. And here's how I would put it: They are single-minded about their goal. So, lesson number one, let nothing and no one derail you in your single-mindedness."*

# JODY CONRADT

*"When we identify successful people, the first quality I look for is commitment, intensity, focus. There are a lot of ways to say it, but it all means that what you do is very important to you, and it shows. And right along with that goes enthusiasm. There's nothing worse than coaching a group of people where there is no enthusiasm. Passion means you love it, and that means that you're going to infuse enthusiasm when you go into a group. You always want to have someone on the bench by you who—when you send them into the game—they could change the momentum. They could bring energy, and they could bring enthusiasm, and that spreads to other members of the team."*

# MEG WHITMAN

*"When I joined my first company out of Harvard Business School, which was Procter & Gamble, I was thrilled to have a job at one of the greatest companies in America, and I was hoping to move up the corporate ladder. But I didn't have giant dreams about what could be accomplished. And you know what I did—I simply said, 'You know, I can only do the very best job I can do. And if I deliver the results, put my head down, and be fun to work with and easy to manage, that's all I can do.'*

*"And what I did over time was deliver the results again and again and again. And I'm a big believer that if you are in the*

*neighborhood of delivering the results, in the neighborhood of good things happening, you will get ahead."*

## CATHIE BLACK

*"Make everything that happens or doesn't happen work for you. Opportunities may not always be obvious but they are there. This is what a success mindset is all about—making things work for you."*

## CHARLOTTE BEERS

*"We think if we work harder and smarter that someone will anoint us, and promotions and big spots will come our way; but there's plenty of data that says it's not going to happen like that . . . It's not about the work: It's about your delivery system. Delivery is the force field around you that gets the work seen, used, and recognized."*

## CATHIE BLACK

*"How do you sustain the success mindset? First, don't take things personally. Women have a graduate degree in taking all things personally. We admit it. We go over it. We repeat it . . .*

"The point is: The sooner that we let a bad day or bad experience go means that we're just that much faster and excited about getting to the next point. It isn't denial. It's sanity, and it's smart."

## JODY CONRADT

"I think the people who are going to be successful are the people who understand how to use the team around them, and through that effort, they still have the ability to show their own individual skills . . . Even as much as we are into technology, I think all of us are dependent on other people to look good. I don't think there's any job where you work totally in isolation, from beginning to end, [where] you're the only person that has an impact."

# 17

# Swear Off Perfectionism: Go for Growth

. . . . . . . . .

# MARCUS BUCKINGHAM

*"If you want to, you can spend your entire life being fixated on everything that is wrong with you: what is wrong with you in terms of your work, what is wrong with you in terms of your relationships. Your entire life can get focused on that. But if you want to have more strength, purpose, and fulfillment in life, you have to begin by deeply understanding what is working in your life. You've got to understand what your strengths are."*

. . . . . . . . . . . .

Marcus, known as the "founder of the strengths revolution," is a British-American *New York Times* best-selling author, thought leader, and motivational speaker. He spent seventeen years at the Gallup Organization researching what distinguishes world's best leaders, managers, and workplaces. In partnership with Gallup, he developed the "StrengthsFinder personality test."

# BRENÉ BROWN

*"Perfectionism is the big shield we carry. It's an addictive way of thinking that says, 'If I look perfect, love perfect, work perfect, and do it all perfectly, I'll be able to avoid judgment and criticism and blame.' The truth is that perfectionism is a 20-ton shield that doesn't protect you from anything. It just keeps you from being seen . . . And it doesn't work."*

# DR. JEN ARNOLD

*"You've got to try, you've got to initiate, you've got to believe. But you also have to continually improve. You know, I think once we achieve certain goals in our lives, it's very easy just to say, 'Okay, I did it. I'm done.' But we can always strive to improve, whether in our personal life, our professional life, or even in our life of helping the world in general. You can improve by going to volunteer at a local shelter.*

*"You can improve just by reaching out to a colleague at work who may be going through a hard time. You can improve by taking more steps to helping out your children. Every day in my profession as a neonatologist, I'm trying to improve the lives of others around us, but it's not always easy. So, you always have to take a step back and say, 'Okay, I've made it this far, but what can I do to do better?'"*

# MARTHA STEWART

*"My little motto, my little mantra every day, is learn something new every day."*

. . . . . . . . . . . .

Martha is an entrepreneur, TV personality, founder of Martha Stewart Living Omnimedia, and the publisher of *Martha Stewart Living* magazine. She is also a best-selling author, most recently of *The Martha Manual: How to Do (Almost) Everything.* As a high school student, she babysat for the children of New York Yankees legends Mickey Mantle and Yogi Berra.

## BRENÉ BROWN

*"I used to live by a quote I have on a little paperweight at home that says 'What would you do if you knew you couldn't fail?' I don't think that's a daring greatly way to live. I think the daring greatly quote is, 'What's worth doing, even if you fail?' Because if we're not willing to be vulnerable, if we're not willing to fail, we can't grow and learn and love."*

## SOLEDAD O'BRIEN

*"Step out of the space that you're in and revel in the discomfort. Dig into those feelings. Ask yourself: Why am I afraid? Why am I uncomfortable? And how can you use that fear to grow? We have so much to accomplish, and we can change lives, starting, frankly, with our own."*

# CANDY CHANG

*"In different stages, our calling evolves and grows. As children, our calling is to play. Then we take in the world. We absorb and explore and experiment. In the next phase of life, we try to become independent, follow our dreams, make a living, be a part of society. And then we try to accept responsibility, nurture our family and relationships, balance work and the other parts of our lives.*

*"But our journey doesn't end there. We continue to learn and grow throughout our entire lives as much as we allow ourselves. A lot of our time is devoted to seeking the right job or reputation or relationship or outward success.*

*"But it's not enough to be psychologically mature. And Carl Jung said, 'It's easier to go to Mars or to the Moon than it is to penetrate one's own being.' And he coined the term individuation, which is a process in which someone becomes who they truly are.*

*"He said, 'On the second half of life, I think the question now becomes who now, apart from your roles, are you? What does your psyche ask of you? And do you have the courage to deconstruct your identity, your urges, your neuroses, your anxieties, your unresolved issues, and explore what you need to explore to grow into your fully realized genuine self?'"*

# 18

# Take Care of You

. . . . . . . . .

## PATRICIA ARQUETTE

*"I think women have gotten so busy taking care of everyone and working that they can't really prioritize themselves. They can't stop and go, 'Wait a second, what's going on here?' I think we need to shift our mentality and see that by taking better care of ourselves economically, legally, by providing ourselves with these protections, we will take better care of our families and the community as a whole."*

## CHRISTY HAUBEGGER

*"I encourage you to take care of yourself because one of the things I've figured out is you can't really pour from an empty cup. And no matter how you do it, fill your own cup up, and give yourself permission to that."*

## GRETCHEN RUBIN

*"It's very important to get some exercise. You do not need to train for the marathon. You do not need to do an hour spin class. This is something like going for a ten- or twenty-minute walk, especially if you can go outside, because just being in the sunshine is going to give you that boost of mood and energy.*

*"Feeling tired is a reason to exercise, not a reason to skip exercise. But here is a secret tip. Let's say you're having a happiness*

emergency, and it's three o'clock, and you're dragging, and you don't have time to take a nap, and you don't have time to go out for a walk. So what can you do to give yourself a quick fix right now?

"All you have to do is jump up and down, especially if people can see you. There's something about getting both feet off the ground. It's childlike, it's energetic, it's kind of goofy. It will give you that quick boost of energy. If you do jumping jacks next to your desk, skip around the room, run down the stairs, hop over a puddle—just this little gesture can really give you a lift."


## SARAH FERGUSON

"Fitness and fit mind-body-soul is what it's about. It's not about fitting into a pair of blue jeans, it's about health. It's about longevity. And it's about seeing your children get married."


## GRETCHEN RUBIN

"In order to be happy, you need to resolve to get enough sleep . . . Many adults are chronically sleep deprived, and you'll talk to people and they'll say, 'Well, I've trained myself to get by on five hours of sleep,' but when scientists study these people, they are quite impaired. A lack of sleep affects your mood, your memory, your immune function, your focus. They even think it contributes to weight gain."

# 19

# Why the World Needs Women Now

. . . . . . . . .

## SALLIE KRAWCHECK

*"It matters to have more women in senior roles in the work-force; it matters to have more women working. It matters because more diverse leadership teams are better leadership teams. They lead to higher returns for companies, lower risk, lower volatility, more client focus, more long-term focus, more innovation, better stockholder returns, and lower gender pay disparity . . . Getting more women into senior leadership roles matters for all women . . . It matters to all families. And it matters to our economic prosperity."*

## ISABEL ALLENDE

*"There is an increasing awareness that there is no hope for peace and no solution for the economic and environmental crises of the world, without the full engagement of women. Empowering women is no longer just a human rights issue; it's an economic issue. It's a survival of the species and of the planet issue."*

## SARA MARTINEZ TUCKER

*"When I was a general assignments reporter in San Antonio, it was women who were the activists in strengthening their schools, in strengthening their communities, in fighting for the rights of their children. When I was at AT&T, it was women who started*

the employee resource groups, organizing conferences for us to be better employees. And now that I run a national not-for-profit, we have fundraisers in over thirty-seven markets in the United States, and it tends to be women organizing these communities."

## CARLY FIORINA

"The data is clear: Women change the world for the better when they are engaged. And it is not just economic opportunity that requires the participation of women. Every problem you can name—conflict, poverty, disease—every problem requires women to be at the center of its solution. That's what the data show."

## RUTH SIMMONS

"So often as women, we're just so delighted to be in the board-room. We're so delighted to have come of age and to be able to lead, that we forget one essential thing—that if we get there, and if we lead in precisely the same way as those who have gone before us, what value do we add? We've got to bring something new to the equation."

# 20

# Write Your Own Story

## BERT JACOBS

*"Your life is your story, and it doesn't last forever. At the beginning of our story, all of us, everybody tells us we need more. We need more stuff. We need more education. We need more money. But as we get older, further along in our story, we all come to the realization that the only thing we need more of is time. Time to do the things that you love and time to be with the people you love. You have to protect your time with your life, because it is your life."*

## CARLY FIORINA

*"Do not let others define you. Do not carry other people's prejudices as your burden. There is lots of bias and prejudice in the world."*

## MARIA HINOJOSA

*"Many, many years ago my father found a job in Chicago. We're from Mexico originally. He never thought he was going to have to come to this country, but the job as a medical doctor that he expected in Mexico fell through when there was a change in government, et cetera, et cetera, et cetera. So, suddenly, we had to change our lives. I was a year and a half old, the youngest of four. My father had moved to Chicago, and my mother was*

*on a plane with four kids under seven. Right there, she already deserves kudos, but okay.*

*"There were also no direct flights from Mexico City to Chicago at that point. So, we arrived in Dallas. That was where we went through immigration. When that happened, my mother, who is smaller than me, with four kids—and I'm the baby in her arms—she gets to the immigration official, a tall Texan in Dallas. Forgive my accent, but he says, 'Well, ma'am, everybody can pass except for this little baby. She's got a rash, so I'm going to have to put her into quarantine. She's going to have to stay here.'*

*"My mother, somehow with her broken English, found her voice. I don't know exactly what she said or how she said it, but she let it be known to this man that under no circumstances was any of her children going to be left behind in Texas. We were all going to be brought into this country.*

*"Somehow this tall Texas immigration official said, 'Yes, ma'am.' I learned to own my voice. It took a long time, especially when you're a women of color in this country, especially when you're a Latina. You self-doubt a lot. But she, my mother, taught me how to own that voice, and I hope I can inspire others."*

· · · · · · · · · · · ·

Maria is an Emmy-winning journalist, anchor, and executive producer of the Peabody Award–winning show *Latino USA*, which is distributed by NPR. She is the founder of Futuro Media and author most recently of *Raising Raul: Adventures Raising Myself and My Son*. She was born in Mexico City and since 1995 has been named three times as one of the 100 Most Influential Hispanics by *Hispanic Business* magazine for her work as a reporter for CBS, NPR, and CNN.

## SOLEDAD O'BRIEN

"In the twenty-seven years that I've been a journalist, I really learned the power of telling your own story, and leveraging your own voice, even when people don't necessarily care about hearing it. Because our stories are important. They can be inspirational, sometimes they can be a cautionary tale, but they provide a road map for a lot of women who are trying to figure it out, who are coming behind us, and those of us who've been in the game for a moment.

"I think we owe it to others to lay out that path. And whether we got it right, or we got it wrong, or if, more likely, our stories and our journeys are a combination of some stuff we got right and a lot of mistakes that we made, and a bunch of lucky breaks, and opportunities that were taken, and chances that were blown—we have to share our experiences, authentically for others."

# ESMERALDA SANTIAGO

*"Life kept moving and it kept rolling and I kept doing things and I kept dreaming, and I kept expecting that moment when something would say, 'This is it, this is it, this is the thing that you are meant to do the rest of your life.' And it happened at three in the morning when I was thirty-four or thirty-five years old, nursing my child, my first child.*

*"As I'm watching this little kid just days old, I looked at him, and I said, 'He will never know his mother because she doesn't know who she is. She knows she's Puerto Rican. She knows she's this particular age. She's done all these things. But she's not any of those things. Who is she?' And that moment was my epiphany moment, it was the moment when I realized I have to tell this child who his mother is. I have to create the person that is going to raise this child."*

Esmeralda is a memoirist, novelist, and former actress. Oprah called her first memoir, *When I Was a Puerto Rican,* one of the best of a generation. Her second, *Almost a Woman,* was adapted into a film for *Masterpiece Theatre.* She immigrated to the United States at the age of thirteen and, after teaching herself English, graduated from Harvard University and Sarah Lawrence College. In her early sixties, she had a stroke and lost the ability to read. She taught herself English again. She is co-founder with her husband of CANTOMEDIA, an award-winning documentary production company.

# VIOLA DAVIS

"My intention in going into a room as a producer now—as someone who has made it my mission to change how women of color are perceived in my profession—is to come into the room perfectly imperfect. I find that if I come into the room and if I have already owned my story, shame can't exist. When you want nothing from someone else, when you don't want their approval, they can't give you anything at this point other than give you a little bit of money to support your projects. What I found is that everything that I've ever experienced in my life is a part of my strength. That's it. It truly is that simple."

# RUTH SIMMONS

"Pay attention to who you are as a person. Don't sell that out for any reason. It's not worth it. Fight for who you are."

# BERTICE BERRY

"When you walk with purpose, you collide with destiny."

# VIOLA DAVIS

*"Before I got married, I kept having dreams about death . . . I remember telling my therapist, 'Oh my God, I'm getting married and I keep having dreams about death. What does that mean?' She said, 'Well, you sort of are dying to yourself.' And that's how I see my life. It's a dying to self. It's a dying to old ways. It's a dying to other people's perceptions of you and who you really are. It's a dying to everybody who tried to define who I am, even as a black woman.*

*"'You're strong.' 'You're strong all the time.'*

*"'No, I'm not. Sometimes I'm strong.'*

*"'Oh wow, you're really in control of everything. You have all the answers all the time. You know black women are different that way.'*

*"'No, we're not.'*

*"'You've got to be a size two or size zero because otherwise, people are not going to believe you're in a sex scene.'*

*"Oh no, come on. There are 324 million people in this country. Fifty or 51 percent of them are women, and we are not all a size zero or two, but we do very well in our sex lives. No, no, and no.*

*"So, that is my sweet elixir that I offer you: Make yourself known. Own it. That is how we connect, and that is where we find our true belonging . . . And remember, in all of it, ultimately, is grace, and it meets you where you are and it doesn't leave you how it found you."*

# BRENÉ BROWN

*"We've got to dare greatly. We've got to show up and be seen. These are hard times. Don't play small. Don't do that to yourself, and don't do it to the rest of us who need you and your voice."*

# ABOUT THE TEXAS CONFERENCE FOR WOMEN

**The Texas Conference for Women** is a nonpartisan, nonprofit organization with a mission to promote, communicate, and amplify the influence of women in the workplace and beyond. It was founded in 2000 and has attracted more than 100,000 women and men to its annual conferences during its first two decades.

This event is part of what has become the largest network of women's conferences in the United States, which includes the Massachusetts Conference for Women, the Pennsylvania Conference for Women, and the Watermark Conference for Women Silicon Valley. The four conferences attract approximately 45,000 people a year.

In response to growing demand for the information, inspiration, and community offered at these events, the Texas Conference for Women in 2019 introduced a new opening event night preceding the main day conference. It also recently launched year-round digital content offerings that feature in-depth conversations with top-rated speakers on themes including leadership, entrepreneurship, work-life balance, and other issues of interest to working women.

You can learn more at www.TXConferenceforWomen.org, and join the online community and conversation on one of these four platforms:

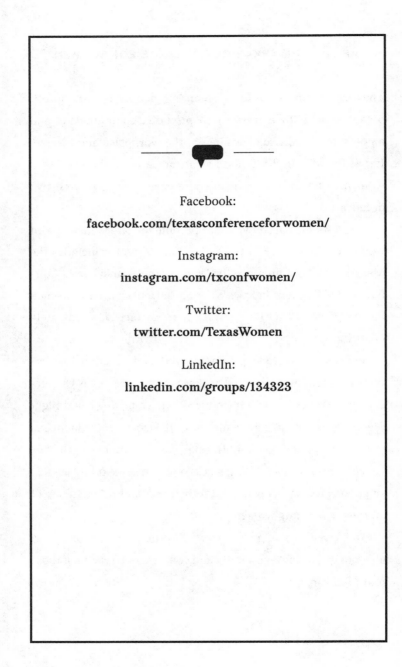

Facebook:

**facebook.com/texasconferenceforwomen/**

Instagram:

**instagram.com/txconfwomen/**

Twitter:

**twitter.com/TexasWomen**

LinkedIn:

**linkedin.com/groups/134323**

## ABOUT THE EDITOR

**Lisa Bennett** is the Communications Director for the Conferences for Women. She is co-author with emotional and social intelligence expert Daniel Goleman of *Ecoliterate* and has contributed to many other books, including *The Compassionate Instinct*, *Smart by Nature*, and *A Place at the Table*. A former Harvard University fellow and Ashoka Changemakers thought leader, her writing awards include the Virginia Center for the Creative Arts Fellowship, Marion Weber Healing Arts Fellowship, and Diversity in Journalism Award.

. . . . . . . . .

# END NOTES

1. Gloria Steinem, "Keynote Speech" (speech, Watermark Conference for Women, San Jose, CA, February 22, 2019).

2. Barbara J. Risman, "Good News! Attitudes Moving Toward Gender Equality," *Psychology Today*, December 17, 2018, https://www.psychologytoday.com/us/blog/gender-questions/201812/good-news-attitudes-moving-toward-gender-equality.

3. Megan Brenan, "Americans No Longer Prefer Male Boss to Female Boss," Gallup, November 16, 2017, https://news.gallup.com/poll/222425/americans-no-longer-prefer-male-boss-female-boss.aspx.

4. "Women and Leadership: 2018," Pew Leadership Center, September 20, 2018, https://www.pewsocialtrends.org/2018/09/20/women-and-leadership-2018/.

5. In 2018, the Pew Research Center found that: "When asked whether men or women in top executive positions are better at creating safe and respectful workplaces, 43% say female executives are better while only 5% say men are better. About half (52%) say male and female leaders are equally capable." Kim Parker, "Many Americans say Women are Better Than Men at Creating Safe, Respectful Workplaces," Pew Research Center, September 25, 2018, https://www.pewresearch.org/fact-tank/2018/09/25/many-americans-say-women-are-better-than-men-at-creating-safe-respectful-workplaces/.

6. Jed Kolko and Claire Cain Miller, "As Labor Market Tightens, Women Are Moving Into Male-Dominated Jobs," *The New York Times*, Dec. 14, 2018, https://www.nytimes.com/2018/12/14/upshot/as-labor-market-tightens-women-are-moving-into-male-dominated-jobs.html.

7. Zameena Mejia, "More Women Entered STEM Over the Past 40 Years Than any Other Field, New Data Shows," CNBC, March 7, 2018, https://www.cnbc.com/2018/03/07/more-women-entered-stem-over-the-past-40-years-than-any-other-field.html.

8. "Women's Wealth is Rising," *The Economist*, March 8, 2018, https://www.economist.com/graphic-detail/2018/03/08/womens-wealth-is-rising.

9. "Financial Facts for Women's History Month," Shurwest, March 14, 2017, http://shurwest.com/2017/03/14/financial-facts-womens-history-month/.

10. Nikki Graf, Anna Brown, and Eileen Patten, "The Narrowing, but Persistent, Gender Gap in Pay," Pew Research Center, March 22, 2019, https://www.pewresearch.org/fact-tank/2019/03/22/gender-pay-gap-facts/.

11. "EEOC Select Task Force on the Study of Harassment in the Workplace," US Equal Employment Opportunity Commission, https://www.eeoc.gov/eeoc/task_force/harassment.

12. "Women in the Workplace," McKinsey & Company and Lean In, 2018, https://womenintheworkplace.com/?gclid=EAIaIQobChMI0t_ywJuM4gIVkMDACh2CywlCEAAYASAAEgK6XfD_BwE.

13. Emily Bazelon, "A Seat at the Head of the Table," *The New York Times Magazine*, February 21, 2019, https://www.nytimes.com/interactive/2019/02/21/magazine/women-corporate-america.html.

14. "2018 Edelman Earned Brand: Brands Take a Stand," Edelman, October 2018, https://www.edelman.com/sites/g/files/aatuss191/files/2018-10/2018_Edelman_Earned_Brand_Global_Report.pdf.